# THE READING SPECIALIST

# SOLVING PROBLEMS IN THE TEACHING OF LITERACY

Cathy Collins Block, *Series Editor*

*Recent Volumes*

# The Reading Specialist

## Leadership for the Classroom, School, and Community

RITA M. BEAN

THE GUILFORD PRESS
New York    London

© 2004 The Guilford Press
A Division of Guilford Publications, Inc.
72 Spring Street, New York, NY 10012
www.guilford.com

Printed in the United States of America

This book is printed on acid-free paper.

Last digit is print number:  9  8  7  6  5  4  3  2

**Library of Congress Cataloging-in-Publication Data**

Bean, Rita M.
   The reading specialist: leadership for the classroom, school, and
community / by Rita M. Bean.
       p.  cm. — (Solving problems in the teaching of literacy)
Includes bibliographical references and index.
   ISBN 1-57230-982-2 (paper : alk. paper)
   1. Reading teachers—United States. 2. Reading—Remedial
teaching—United States. I. Title. II. Series.
   LB2844.1.R4B43  2004
   372.4—dc22
                                        2003018932

# About the Author

**Rita M. Bean, PhD,** is Professor of Education at the University of Pittsburgh. Prior to joining the University of Pittsburgh, she taught at the elementary school level and also served as a reading supervisor for grades K–12. Dr. Bean has developed elementary and middle school reading curriculum materials and also has published in many different journals and monographs on the topics of reading curriculum, assessment and instruction in reading, and the role of reading specialists.

Dr. Bean directs a reading specialist intern program at the University of Pittsburgh, which places certified teachers in classrooms to serve as reading specialists alongside classroom teachers. She also serves as Director of the Reading Center at the University.

Dr. Bean served as Chair of the International Reading Association's Commission on the Role of the Reading Specialist, which resulted in a position statement approved by the Board, and she is also a member of the Board (2003–2006). In 2002, she received the Chancellor's Distinguished Service Award from the University of Pittsburgh for her community and outreach efforts in improving literacy.

# Acknowledgments

Many individuals have contributed to the ideas in this book, and I wish to acknowledge them for the many ways that they have influenced my thoughts and beliefs about the role of reading specialists.

I thank the members of the International Reading Association's Commission on the Role of the Reading Specialist who worked with me for several years to investigate the status of reading specialists across the United States. Those members include Melinda J. Beckwith, Camille L. Blachowicz, Lillian K. Boyd, Jack Cassidy, Judith Earle Grumet, Rebecca Hamilton, Nelda S. Hensley, Jane Matanzo, Alicia A. Moreyra, Diana J. Quatroche, Dorothy S. Shelton, MaryEllen Vogt, Dave Wallace, and Sandra R. Wallis.

I thank the many students in the reading specialist certification program at the University of Pittsburgh and the reading specialists with whom I have worked who raised questions and concerns about the role of reading specialists, especially as to how they might better meet the needs of struggling readers.

I thank my mentor and colleague, Robert Wilson, Professor Emeritus at the University of Maryland, with whom I coauthored a text that highlighted the importance of the leadership and resource role of reading specialists.

Also many thanks to my secretary, Alberta Asbury, for everything she did to enable me to accomplish the necessary tasks and meet deadlines.

And finally, I thank Tony Eichelberger for his encouragement, critical reading, and constant reminder that there was a need for the message that this book conveyed.

# Preface

*The Reading Specialist* is written for the many reading specialists currently working in schools to improve the reading performance of individual students and the reading program for all students. It is also written for those individuals who are in programs that prepare them to become reading specialists.

The book addresses the many roles that reading specialists at all levels (kindergarten through grade 12) may be asked to assume. My goal was to write a book that offers many practical ideas for those working in the field. I wanted reading specialists to be able to take the book from their bookshelves as a quick resource to use when a particular question or issue arises. At the same time, because the material presented is based on the research and literature related to the work of reading specialists (i.e., instruction, leadership, and assessment), it can be used as a textbook in a reading specialist certification program.

The book focuses on broad issues related to instruction, leadership, and assessment, rather than on the specific issues related to reading content (e.g., teaching decoding or reading comprehension strategies). The major models or approaches for handling the instructional role and the advantages or limitations of a pullout or in-class program are examined. In addition, important dimensions of the leadership role (e.g., conducting professional development, working with community and parents) not usually discussed in general methods books about literacy are explored here.

Many chapters include a question section ("Think about This") to stimulate thinking about various issues discussed in that chapter. At the conclusion of each chapter is a section, "Reflections," that provides more questions for further thought and discussion. A number of activities that may be useful in a course setting or in a study group setting are presented at the end of each chapter.

Also included are vignettes written by three practicing reading specialists who represent the high caliber of exemplary reading specialists working in schools. I thank them for taking the time to write these contributions. The vignettes bring to life the excitement, passion, and commitment of these three dedicated reading specialists.

From the early days of my career, I have been interested and involved in areas of research and teaching that relate to the role of the reading specialist. This book is based on my own experiences as a reading specialist, struggling to meet the needs of students and teachers (K–12). In addition, it is based on my many interactions through the years with other reading specialists faced with similar challenges. Many of the recommendations and ideas for working with others come from the interactions I have had with reading specialists in the field.

During my years at the University of Pittsburgh, I have also been involved in preparing reading specialists. These potential reading specialists have taught me a great deal. They have shared their experiences in schools working with struggling readers and with teachers to improve the reading program. We worked collaboratively to solve the problems that they faced; their voices are present in this book.

Finally, my interactions with other professionals in the field have certainly influenced the contents of this book. The Commission on the Role of the Reading Specialist provided me with many opportunities to listen to the thoughts of reading specialists and those preparing reading specialists across the United States. They too are represented in this book.

The field is a dynamic one; the work of reading specialists has never been more important, given the emphasis on literacy as a key to future success. It is my hope that this book will serve as a resource for reading specialists that will enable them to address questions or issues they face as they strive to improve reading achievement in the schools in which they work.

# Contents

x                        Contents

# 1

# The Role of Reading Specialists in Schools and Classrooms

Every school should have access to specialists . . . reading
specialists who have specialized training related to
addressing reading difficulties and who can give guidance
to classroom teachers.
— SNOW, BURNS, AND GRIFFIN (1998, p. 333)

Much has been learned about how to teach reading to all students, yet the evidence is clear that there are students in our schools
who are not learning to read or who are struggling to learn to read.
Across the United States, legislators, businessmen, parents, and educators alike are searching for ways to address this dilemma. One of the
recommendations is that schools employ reading specialists who can
work with struggling readers as well as provide support to classroom
teachers. This recommendation is found in the report of the National
Research Council (Snow, Burns, & Griffin, 1998), documents of the
International Reading Association, and in the work of researchers
(Allington & Baker, 1999; Bean, Cassidy, Grumet, Shelton, & Wallis,
2002; Bean, Swan, & Knaub, 2003). It is this dual role that is addressed
in this book. This role requires that reading specialists have expertise

with reading assessment and instruction as well as possessing the leadership skills that enable them to work with other adults, such as classroom teachers, other professionals (e.g., speech teachers, special educators), and the community (e.g., parents, volunteers, media personnel). This introductory chapter, which provides an organizational framework for the other chapters, begins with a brief history of the reading specialist in the schools, especially in regard to compensatory programs such as Chapter or Title 1. A discussion of what is known about the role of the reading specialist, based on research in the field, follows.

## WHERE WE HAVE BEEN

The use of specialists dates back to the 1930s when they functioned essentially as supervisors who worked with teachers to improve the reading program. It was after World War II, in response to the raging criticism of the schools and their inability to teach children to read, that "remedial reading teachers" became fixtures in many schools, public and private, elementary through secondary. The primary responsibility of the specialist was to work with individuals or small groups of children who were experiencing difficulty in learning to read. Briggs and Coulter (1977) stated, "Like Topsy, these remedial reading services just 'growed,' aided and abetted by government at all levels and by private foundations quick to provide grants of funding for such programs" (p. 216). Even the International Reading Association (1968), in their "Guidelines for Reading Specialists," strongly supported the remedial role: five of the six functions described for the "special teacher of reading" related directly to instructional responsibilities. However, there were those educators who began to see the difficulty of reading specialists serving only an instructional capacity. Stauffer (1967) described the remedial role as one of working in a "bottomless pit" and supported the idea of the reading specialist serving as a consultant.

Support for reading specialists will be serving in multiple roles continued throughout the next several decades. In 1981, Bean and Wilson wrote about the resource role of the reading specialist, emphasizing the importance of interpersonal, leadership, and communication skills for those in reading specialist positions. However, various factors restricted the roles that reading specialists assumed, including the source of funding that provided support for these specialized personnel, and, indeed, research that contributed to new ideas about reading instruction and assessment.

## Role of Reading Specialists in Compensatory Programs

In the past 30 years, a large percentage of reading specialists was funded by Title 1 of the Elementary and Secondary Education Act (ESEA). This large compensatory program, funded by the federal government, was developed to provide supplemental support to students who were economically deprived. In the initial conceptualization of this program, policies and procedures were developed to ensure that the appropriate students were receiving support provided by these funds. Reading specialists who were funded by Title 1 funds were therefore required to work only with eligible students and to purchase and use various resources and materials for those students only. Such policies led to what is commonly referred to as "pullout" programs, large, separate, and distinct programs for designated students.

These programs generated many problems. There was little congruence or alignment between the classroom program and the supplemental program, so students received two different programs, with no "bridges" connecting them. Some reading specialists were not knowledgeable about the instruction students were receiving in their classrooms (Allington, 1986; Slavin, 1987), nor did they share what they were doing with the classroom teachers! Moreover, when students who received Title 1 services typically returned to their classrooms, they were then asked to learn from materials that were too difficult for them or to use strategies or skills different from those they were learning in their pullout program. Another problem was that, too often, students in these supplemental programs spent their time doing workbook-type, skill-related activities. There was little opportunity to read nor was there much direct instruction (Allington & McGill-Franzen, 1989; Bean, Cooley, Eichelberger, Lazar, & Zigmond, 1991). Some classroom teachers seemed to think that the reading specialists were responsible for teaching these students to read, even though the instruction provided by the specialists was identified as *supplemental*.

At the same time, teachers resented the "swinging-door" dimension of pullout programs; their instruction was interrupted by students coming into and going out of their classrooms. This feeling is illustrated in an article from a newsletter published by a teachers' organization:

> Over the past few months I've been noticing that my class has been quietly disappearing. They leave one by one, or in small groups. They come late due to dentist appointments and leave early for eye exams.

They are being remediated, enriched, guided, weighed, and measured. They are leaving me to learn to speak English, pass the TELLS test, increase sight vocabulary, develop meaningful relationships, and to be PEP'd or BEEP'd.

They slip in and out with such frequency that I rarely have my whole class together for any length of time on any given day. I don't know when to schedule a test anymore. I've considered administering them during lunch when I'm on cafeteria duty—but then again the "packers" aren't sitting with the "buyers"—so we are still not all together.

One day I accidentally had the whole class in my room. As soon as I discovered it, I quickly gave them their language pretest and posttest! If it ever happens again, they're getting their final exam.

When the office calls for one of my students, I try to be fair about it. My policy is—if they can find them, they can have them. I find you can get one small advantage from all this coming and going, if you work it right. You seat your talkative kids in between the frequent remedials and half the time they'll be next to empty desks.

I am learning to deal with the disappearances. I teach in bits and pieces to parts of the whole. But you can help me out, if you will. If you even run into any of my meandering students, say "hi" for me—and take them over their time tables please. (Anonymous, 1986)

Another problem was the stigma associated with leaving the classroom; students were viewed by their peers as being dumb or different, creating a lack of self-esteem in these students. Allington (1986) and others were concerned that pullout programs that provided minimal reading instruction (e.g., 35–40 minutes, several times a week) did not address the serious needs of students.

The results of large-scale evaluations of Title or Chapter 1 were not always positive, although Borman and D'Agostine (2001), in their meta-analysis of Title 1 program effects, indicated that "there has been a positive trend for the educational effectiveness of Title 1 across the years of its operation" (p. 49). They contended that, without these services, students would have fallen further behind academically. The evaluation of Title 1 has been difficult because it is essentially a funding program, and there are many variations in the ways that it is implemented in districts across this nation. At the same time, the great expectation for Title 1— that it close the achievement gap between at-risk, poor students and their more advantaged peers—has not been met.

Many changes were recommended in the literature and in the new legislation of 1988. These changes included recommendations for additional collaboration with classroom teachers and special educators and more emphasis on programs in which reading specialists worked in the classrooms with teachers. These recommendations certainly influenced the role of reading specialists, making it essential that they be able to work well with other adults.

## Changes in Reading Assessment and Instruction

In the early days of Title programs, reading specialists carefully documented the reading achievement and reading expectancy of students who might be eligible for compensatory services. Reading expectancy was calculated in various ways, from obtaining the intelligence quotient of the students to administering a listening comprehension test. Teacher judgment, at times, was used. Only those students who were identified as "discrepant"—that is, their test performance revealed a gap between achievement and potential—were assigned to receive reading services. With growing recognition of (1) the limitations inherent in scores achieved on intelligence and standardized tests and (2) possible test bias in identifying students, the use of a discrepancy formula was eliminated, and students were identified based upon their actual reading achievement.

This criticism of standardized testing also led to the identification of new indicators of success for students and Title 1 programs, with a primary emphasis on how well students performed on "authentic" measures and indicators of success in the classroom. Schools, therefore, have recently found themselves in the position of creating their own measures, identifying what they want students to know and be able to do at various grade levels. Often, reading specialists find themselves in the position of working with classroom teachers to develop such instruments.

Likewise, changes in reading instruction have influenced the work of reading specialists. As mentioned previously, Allington and Shake (1986) and Bean and colleagues (1991), who studied Chapter 1 programs, found that reading specialists often spent their time using "skill and drill" methods. Students completed worksheets or participated in specialized programs that emphasized skill instruction. Little time was spent on reading itself. Yet research evidence and theorists in the field were advocating the teaching of more explicit reading strategies and increased opportunities for students to engage actively in reading and writing tasks.

## WHERE WE ARE

The changes described previously and the evaluations of Title 1 led to a period in the 1990s when school districts eliminated or downsized the number of reading specialists in their schools. One reading specialist summarized the situation as follows:

> Our grant from Title 1 is substantial; yet rather than use the expertise of reading specialists in the district's reading program, the number of specialists has dropped in the last several years from 14 to 4. Reading Specialists have been assigned to classroom teaching positions or have not been replaced from attrition. Blame for dropping reading scores has been laid at the Title 1 door; reading specialists are an expensive liability. Reading specialists are being replaced with many, many inexpensive aides. (personal communication, 1991)

Various programs and strategies were implemented to address the problems of struggling readers: increasing the competence of classroom teachers, reducing class size, using technology in the classrooms, adding after-school and summer programs, employing volunteers and aides to work with students. All of these strategies, though they can be beneficial, did not seem to produce the desired results, however.

In 1995 the International Reading Association, encouraged by its members, established a commission to investigate the role and status of reading specialists in schools. The commission was given three tasks: (1) analyze the literature and research about the role of the specialist, (2) conduct a survey of members to determine what reading specialists were actually doing in schools, and (3) investigate the role of reading specialists in exemplary schools. This work is reported in three articles found in *The Reading Teacher* (Bean, Cassidy, et al., 2002; Bean, Swan, & Knaub, 2003; Quatroche, Bean, & Hamilton, 2001). Some of the key findings of the commission are reported below. The work resulted in a position statement, *Teaching All Children to Read: The Roles of the Reading Specialist* (International Reading Association, 2000; see Appendix A).

## National Survey of Reading Specialists

The survey of reading specialists (Bean, Cassidy, et al., 2002) revealed interesting and, in some ways, disturbing information. Completed questionnaires were returned by 1,517 individuals who identified themselves as reading specialists. The respondents were 97% white and 98% female; they were also experienced educators, with 86% having served as classroom teachers. More than 90% worked directly with students on a daily basis, providing instructional services either in the classroom or on a pullout basis. Interestingly, pullout instruction was still prevalent, although respondents indicated that one of the changes they saw in their position was a move to more in-class instruction. Most reading specialists worked with primary grade students. Respondents also reported a greater expectation that reading specialists function as a resource to teachers and that they plan instruction for students with classroom teachers on a regular basis.

One of the disturbing findings of the survey was the virtual absence of men and minority groups among the reading specialist population, a problematic finding given the need to provide good role models for students who themselves may be male or from a minority group. Likewise, the lack of specialists at the intermediate, middle school, and high school levels reduces the potential for maintaining performance of students and helping content teachers at those levels understand how they can help students read informational text more effectively. Finally, although respondents did indicate that they planned lessons with teachers, many also indicated that they had little time for planning because they were scheduled to teach large numbers of students almost every period of the day.

## Reading Specialists in Exemplary Schools

The study by Bean, Swan, and Knaub (2003) provided the most provocative information about the role of the specialists. First, principals in the exemplary schools selected were extremely positive about the importance of the reading specialist to the success of their reading program, with 97% indicating that specialists were "extremely" or "very important" to its success. These specialists were experienced teachers (all but one of them worked directly with students), all of them also served in a leadership role, and all of them saw the leadership role as an essential part of their work. These specialists also identified the following capacities and qualities that they believed characterize the ideal reading specialist:

- Teaching ability
- Knowledge of reading instruction
- Sensitivity to children with reading difficulties
- Knowledge of assessments
- Ability and willingness to fill an advocacy role
- Ability to work with adults
- Knowledge of reading research
- Perceive themselves as lifelong learners
- Ability to provide professional development
- Ability to articulate reading philosophy
- Energy

*Think about This*

Which capacities and qualities do you believe are most important? Why?

The position statement adopted by the Board of Directors, International Reading Association, calls for reading specialists to apply their expertise in the areas of assessment, instruction, and leadership (Figure 1.1). In the following chapters, the role played by reading specialists in each of those areas is explored and ideas for working effectively are provided.

## WHERE WE ARE GOING

There are several movements in today's schools that may affect the roles of the reading specialist. First, the current emphasis on reading has led to a call for better qualified and prepared teachers—and with that call comes support for well-prepared individuals who can serve as coaches or mentors for teachers in the schools. These individuals would need to have an in-depth knowledge of reading instruction and assessment as well as the skills to work effectively with other adults. Certainly, many reading specialists have these abilities and skills and may find themselves in such a position. Some may serve only as coaches whereas oth-

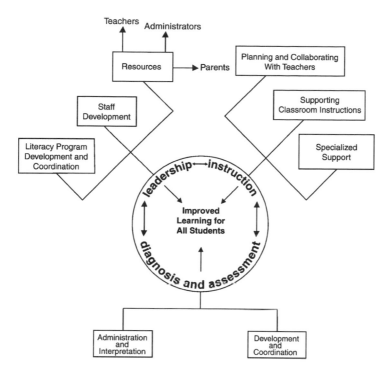

**FIGURE 1.1.** Graphic from the International Reading Association; IRA (2000, September). Teaching all children to read: The roles of the reading specialist. *The Reading Teacher,* 54(1), 115–119. Copyright 2000 by the International Reading Association. Reprinted by permission.

ers may find themselves in a dual role, teaching students and serving as a resource for teachers.

The present focus on research-based reading instruction has implications for reading specialists. As schools move to implement research findings, it is critical to have individuals in place who have an understanding of the research and can interpret what the findings mean for reading instruction. With this emphasis on research-based reading instruction comes a call for accountability. Schools are being asked not only to implement appropriate classroom instructional practices, but they must also show that the instruction has had an effect on student performance in reading. Again, the impact on the role of reading specialists is evident: They must understand how to assess reading growth, interpret results, and communicate results to others.

The concern about reading achievement at all levels, especially with the standards movement that may require students to pass various literacy tests at middle school and high school levels, is generating interest in placing reading specialists at those levels. These specialists will need skills that enable them to work effectively not just with teachers of reading but with content area teachers, since it is in those areas that reading specialists need to focus if they are to help students achieve success.

The concern about students' literacy skills has generated a great deal of focus on the instruction that goes on in preschool and day-care settings. There has been a call for better preparation of preschool teachers and for better transitional programs bridging preschool and kindergarten (Snow, Burns, & Griffin, 1998). In turn, these issues call for well-prepared reading specialists who can work cooperatively with preschool educators so that there is a better understanding of what students need to know and do when they arrive in kindergarten—and so that kindergarten teachers have a better idea of what students are learning in preschool settings. This movement also calls for more partnering among all individuals and agencies involved in the education of young children: parents, teachers, preschools, libraries, community agencies. The reading specialist in tomorrow's schools needs to be prepared to work effectively with all these groups.

## SUMMARY

The role of the reading specialist has continued to evolve over the past decades. Currently, we are experiencing a greater emphasis on the leadership or resource role. Some of these changes have occurred in response to research findings on reading instruction and assessment practices. Other changes have emerged on the heels of criticism about the results of compensatory programs, which lacked congruence between classroom and supplemental instruction. New emphases in reading instruction and increased demand for scientifically based reading instruction will create demands for reading specialists to assume an increased leadership role. Reading specialists, however, will continue to fill multiple roles that require individuals with an in-depth knowledge of reading instruction and assessment and the ability to work well with other adults.

## Reflections

1. What skills and abilities do you think are essential for working successfully as a reading specialist in an instructional role? Leadership role? Assessment role?
2. With which of the roles are you most comfortable? What concerns do you have about the other roles?
3. What are the implications of the following issues for reading specialists and their role: placement in the middle or secondary school, increased emphasis on working with preschool providers, focus on research-based reading instruction, and focus on accountability?

## Activities

1. Analyze your own skills in relation to the three areas of expertise required of reading specialists: assessment, instructional, and leadership. Write a summary of your thoughts, indicating your strengths and where you think you may need to gain additional experience or knowledge.
2. Interview a reading specialist, asking questions about how he or she fulfills responsibilities in the following areas: instruction, assessment, and leadership. You may want to use the questions in the following section.

## Interviewing Reading Specialists

1. What are your responsibilities as a reading specialist? (Ask the person to describe what he or she does in his or her school/program.)
2. How do you determine the goals and content of your instruction? (Ascertain *what* determines the instruction—and who.)
3. Which assessment instruments do you find to be particularly helpful in diagnosing your students' needs?
4. How do you use assessment results?
5. In what ways do you serve as a resource to teachers?
6. If you were able to develop your own assessment program, what would you emphasize or change?
7. What are some of the major difficulties experienced by your students?
8. What are the major issues you face as a reading specialist?

# 2

# An Overview of the Instructional Role

Although reading specialists have multiple roles, one of the key roles is that of instructor, working with students who are struggling with reading. There are many students in our schools who need additional or supplemental support by teachers who have specialized training. Moreover, as mentioned in several studies, reading specialists themselves value the instructional role (Bean, Cassidy, et al., 2002; Bean, Swan, & Knaub, 2003). Working with students can enable reading specialists to gain a better understanding of what is occurring in the classroom and help them establish credibility with teachers. This chapter discusses approaches that have been used successfully by reading specialists in working with struggling readers—from working in pullout programs to working with teachers in the classroom.

There is no single model of the instructional role for reading specialists to follow. Those who work in Title 1 programs may find themselves in classrooms, in pullout models, or both. Those at middle school and secondary levels often focus on reading in the content areas, and although they frequently work in the classroom with teachers, they may also have responsibility for a class of students needing supplemental reading support. Often reading specialists work with small groups of children; however, there are also specialized programs such as Reading Recovery (Clay, 1985) and Success for All (Slavin, Madden, Dolan, & Wasik, 1996) that require individual instruction or tutoring of students.

## WHAT READING SPECIALISTS NEED TO KNOW ABOUT WORKING IN AN INSTRUCTIONAL ROLE

### Need for Collaboration

Regardless of the approach and where the instruction is being delivered, it is critical that reading specialists communicate and collaborate with the teacher who is providing the "first" instruction to students. Only if the reading specialist knows what the classroom teacher is doing, and vice versa, can the most appropriate instruction be provided for students. Much has been learned about the problems that typically arise when struggling readers are faced with fragmented instruction that only increases their confusion—and dismay. Likewise, adjustments need to be made so that these readers are not asked to do both the work required by the classroom teacher and the reading specialist. Students should not be made to stay in during recess or take assignments home because they did not complete the work required by the classroom teacher (because they were receiving instruction from the reading specialist).

Reading specialists and classroom teachers have been ingenious in finding ways to communicate and collaborate. Often this is done "on the fly," since schools do not provide the time essential for such planning. Indeed, this lack of collaborative planning time was one of the greatest concerns of reading specialists who participated in the national survey conducted by the Commission on the Role of the Reading Specialist (Bean, Cassidy, et al., 2002). Ogel and Fogelberg (2001) asked reading specialists to describe a successful collaboration and the reasons for its success. The respondents identified, among other factors, the need for an effective school climate or culture that permits teachers to experiment with new ways of teaching. Creating environments that facilitate and reward collaboration among educators, thereby promoting learning communities, is the ideal. In the following sections, I discuss practical ideas for promoting collaboration.

## WRITTEN COMMUNICATION

Simple forms that can be completed by both teachers and reading specialists enable them to determine quickly what is being emphasized by each venue in a particular week or unit. These forms also serve as a paper trail that can be useful in decision making as well as to provide detailed information to parents and other educators (see Figure 2.1). Some teachers actually share or exchange copies of lesson plans. Reading specialists can ask teachers to identify the skills or strategies they are working on that week and can plan their lessons to coincide with them.

## ORAL COMMUNICATION

### Scheduled Meetings

School districts have designed many different approaches to providing needed planning time for teachers and reading specialists. For example, specialists may meet with grade level or subject area teachers once a week during a designated planning period. Teachers discuss common needs, particular issues, and students who may need supplemental help. One of the advantages of these meetings is that teachers learn from each other when they share ideas; such meetings also tend to encourage teamwork among teachers and specialists.

Some districts hire a substitute to manage a classroom for one period for each participating teacher, and the reading specialist meets with individual teachers during the entire day. This approach, because of its cost, tends to be used only once a month or even less frequently.

Reading specialists also meet with individual teachers either before or after school, during a designated time for teacher planning/preparation. However, some teachers may be reluctant to give up this time during which they plan for the following day.

### Informal Conversations

There may be opportunities to talk briefly when students are working independently. However, this is not an approach that allows for long periods of discussion, since teachers need to be available to assist—and watch—as students are working. Many times teachers talk informally during their lunch break or in the halls. Knaub (2002), in her study of

Teacher: _____  Grade:_____

What story are you reading?_____

What are the key words being taught? (Attach list, if available.)_____

_____

Are you working on any specific skills or strategies?_____

What letters/sounds are being taught?_____

Do you need me to help you with something special when I come in for in-class
instruction?_____

_____

What day would be best for our in-class session?_____

Do you need help with a specific lesson? (Identify.)_____

Are there any students about whom you have concerns?_____

Anything else?

FIGURE 2.1. Coordination Form.

collaborative work between specialists and classroom teachers, found that teachers and reading specialists who worked together became familiar with various types of lessons (e.g., Cunningham & Hall's [1994] *Making Words*) and were able to coordinate their teaching effectively and with little planning. Knaub coined the phrase "impromptu planning" to convey the ease with which reading specialists and teachers often collaborate.

## Need for Support from Administration

Without administrative support, there is less chance that meaningful collaboration will occur. Schedules that provide teachers and reading specialists with opportunities to plan and policies and procedures that encourage collaboration are necessary for developing an effective program. Likewise, reading specialists need schedules that enable them to be in specific classrooms during the teaching of appropriate subjects. Even the placement of students needs to be considered carefully. As noted by Ogle and Fogelberg (2001), reading specialists cannot be in all classrooms to serve children; thus struggling readers may need to be placed in two or three classrooms so that they can receive services from the reading specialist. Administrators can also show their support by providing staff development for all teachers participating in collaborative teaching. It is not sufficient for reading specialists alone to understand how to work collaboratively; all teachers can benefit from experiences that heighten their understanding of what collaboration means and how to do it.

## Need for Clear Procedures

Both classroom teachers and reading specialists must know and understand their roles in the classroom, else the lack of clear procedures leads to problems. Reading specialists may feel as though they have no clear instructional responsibility and therefore "float" around the classroom, trying to anticipate what might be helpful. This type of role seems to generate the feeling in reading specialists that they are "aides" in the classroom and that their expertise is not used or valued. Classroom teachers also experience frustration because they do not know exactly why the reading specialist is even present. Only with the establishment of clear expectations can teachers both enjoy and recognize the benefit of an additional person in their classrooms. However, establishing those clear expectations is not easy, given the culture that has existed in schools in which each teacher is assigned a group of students and is responsible for the academic success of those students. Teachers are accustomed to teaching in isolated settings, planning and implementing instruction that they deem best. Figure 2.2 identifies questions that the classroom teacher and reading specialist can ask each other as they think about how to work together.

*Think about This*

Would you feel comfortable using the questions in Figure 2.2 in a conversation with teachers? How can you use these questions effectively?

The following scenario describes how a reading specialist and a third-grade teacher planned their lessons for a week, using a framework that builds on the materials that are being used in the classroom.

The schedule calls for the reading specialist to be in this classroom for only 3 days a week, Monday, Wednesday, and Friday, for 30 minutes. This week, the class is reading the selection *Mom Can't See Me* by Sally Alexander. The classroom teacher introduces the selection on Monday, focusing on vocabulary and prior knowledge. Because students are working with vocabulary in small groups, both the reading specialist and teacher circulate to help students (the reading specialist is present only during the time that the students work in groups).

On Tuesday, the entire class reads the selection together and participates in a discussion with the classroom teacher.

On Wednesday, the goal is fluency practice; three groups are formed, with the reading specialist working with one group, the classroom teacher with another. The third group is engaging in partner reading. The reading specialist asks students in his or her group to read various sections of the selection, often using the technique of "echo" reading. He or she also reviews some of the concepts and understandings that were addressed in the discussion during the previous day. Students in the teacher's group also read orally, but this group is focused on finding and reading parts of the selection that answer specific comprehension questions.

On Thursday, the teacher presents a specific skill suggested in the anthology to the entire class and introduces a writing task to

|  | Yes | No |
|---|---|---|
| 1. Do we come to class with prepared materials/ideas? | ___ | ___ |
| 2. Do we signal our students to come to us when it is time? | ___ | ___ |
| 3. Do we follow through on plans made at joint planning sessions? | ___ | ___ |
| 4. Do we provide feedback on students' lessons to other teachers regularly and frequently? | ___ | ___ |
| 5. Do we compliment the instruction we see? | ___ | ___ |
| 6. Do we bring materials to joint planning sessions? | ___ | ___ |
| 7. Do we share new strategies with the other teachers? | ___ | ___ |
| 8. Do we engage in self-reflection after teaching a lesson? | ___ | ___ |
| 9. Do classroom teachers try to help the reading specialist "fit in" with the flow of the classroom? | ___ | ___ |
| 10. Do we invite feedback on students/lessons from each other? | ___ | ___ |
| 11. Do classroom teachers share expectations for student behavior? | ___ | ___ |
| 12. Do we try to keep to a schedule? (Does the reading specialist arrive on time? Does the teacher plan to be ready for the collaborative lesson?) | ___ | ___ |
| 13. Do we discuss other classroom teachers/reading specialists or students with others in a professional manner? | ___ | ___ |
| 14. Do we "keep up" on reading instruction information and read professional journals? | ___ | ___ |
| 15. Do we demonstrate respect for the other teachers? | ___ | ___ |

**FIGURE 2.2.** Classroom Teacher/Reading Specialist Self-Reflection Questionnaire.

the students: "Write a letter to the author telling [her] what you liked about the story and raising questions that you would like to have her answer."

On Friday, students continue to write the letter and they are also given time to read additional materials that are available in the classroom. The reading specialist and teacher are holding conferences with students, helping them to think about what they have written and how they might revise or edit their work. The focus is on writing a friendly letter to an author. For 10 minutes, the reading specialist also works with a small group to review a specific decoding skill, which he or she and the teacher had noted was causing these students difficulty.

This reading specialist and teacher use a mutually agreed-upon framework in planning each week's lesson. The specialist knows that he or she is going to help students as they work with vocabulary on Mondays (she may also create a small group to do some review work); on Wednesdays, the focus is on rereading the selection, and the reading specialist often works with the group experiencing the most difficulty; on Fridays, there is an emphasis on some follow-up activity (e.g., writing, art, or creative dramatics). The reading specialist assists with this activity, or he or she may work with a small group to provide additional reading practice or review specific strategies or skills. This set of procedures is, of course, only one way that two teachers may work together. Many different approaches can be used; the approach selected may depend upon the curricular demands or the needs of the students.

---

*Think about This*

What do you see as the strengths of this framework? Do you have any concerns about it? What skills and abilities do the reading specialist and classroom teacher need to make this framework effective? What other procedures do you think might work?

---

## APPROACHES TO COLLABORATION

In this section, I describe five approaches to collaboration that are based on the literature (Bean, Trovato, & Hamilton, 1995; Cook & Friend,

1995; Hamilton, 1993) and on observations made of reading specialist interns and classroom teachers (Bean, Grumet, & Bulazo, 1999). Some of the approaches require in-class teaching, whereas others might occur either in class or away from the classroom; all require collaborative planning. Table 2.1 provides a summary of the approaches and lists the advantages as well as potential problems of each (Bean, 2001).

## Station or Center Teaching

Both reading specialists and teachers can develop stations or centers for teaching, based on the needs of the students and their own expertise or interests. For example, the classroom teacher might be responsible for a center on writing, while the reading specialist guides a review center for phonics or vocabulary development. This method enables both teachers to work with all students as they rotate through the centers. Such centers can be used two or three times a week, thereby facilitating a flexible, heterogeneous grouping of students. One of the advantages of learning centers is that teachers can design activities for areas of literacy in which they have specific expertise or interest. They can also focus their energies on a specific area of reading, thus reducing preparation time. To implement these centers effectively, teachers need to have excellent organizational and classroom management skills. Furthermore, both teachers have to work collaboratively. Some teachers may have difficulty with the noise level that occurs in their classrooms as the centers are functioning. Although the materials for centers may take extra time to prepare, once developed, they are available for future use.

## Support Teaching

The support teaching approach to collaboration is generally based on student needs, with the reading specialist (generally, but not always) working with students who may require additional review or reteaching of a particular skill or strategy. Students who need additional exposure to the vocabulary of a story (perhaps even before the story is introduced) may be grouped for instruction, while other students work on their writing projects or do independent reading. Likewise, the teachers may plan to conduct small-group work, with one teacher overseeing the oral reading of the selection while other students read the selection silently. Some students may be pulled for individual instruction. In one school district, reading specialists take primary children for short 10-

**TABLE 2.1. Models of Collaboration**

| Model | Advantages | Potential problems/dilemmas | Location |
|---|---|---|---|
| Station or center teaching | Students have opportunity to work with both teachers<br>Attention to individual/group needs or interests<br>Small-group work<br>Teachers have some choice (utilizes teacher strengths and interests)<br>Teachers share responsibility for developing and teaching | Time consuming to develop<br>Noise level in classroom<br>Organizational factors<br>Management factors | In class |
| Support teaching | Focuses on individual or group needs<br>Small-group instruction<br>Specialized instruction<br>Utilizes talents of teachers to meet needs of students | The need to know both classroom reading program and specialized approaches<br>Rigid grouping | Either in class or pullout |
| Parallel instruction | Pacing/approach can vary<br>Small-group instruction<br>Same standards/expectations for all students<br>Easier to handle class | May not meet needs of students<br>Noise level | Generally in class (can be pullout) |
| Teach and monitor | Same standards/expectations for all students<br>Immediate reinforcement or help from monitor<br>Opportunity to do "kid watching" (assessment)<br>Teachers can learn from each other (demonstration) | One teacher may feel reduced to aide status<br>Lack of attention to specific needs of children | In class |
| Team teaching | Same standards/expectations for all students<br>Utilizes strengths of both teachers<br>Teachers share responsibility<br>Students have opportunity to work with both teachers<br>Attention to individual/group needs or interests<br>Small-group work | Lack of common philosophy or approach to instruction | Generally in class |

*Note.* From Bean (2001, p. 357). Copyright 2001 by the International Reading Association. Reprinted by permission.

minute mini-lessons, asking them to read orally, working with a word or words that present difficulty for them, and then providing opportunities for students to compose a sentence that can be read, cut into strips, reordered, reread, and taken home for practice (along with the book that has been read).

## Parallel Instruction

Parallel instruction provides opportunities for reducing the size of the class. Both teachers cover the same lesson and the same content but with a different group of students. Such instruction enables teachers to change the pace and the instructional techniques, depending on the needs of the students. For example, both teachers may focus on comprehension, using the same materials, but teach in ways that reflect the different needs of the students. In one group, the teacher may move quickly through the story and focus on the comprehension strategies that enhance students' understanding of the selection after the reading. In the other group, more time may be spent on helping students use prediction to develop their readiness to read the story. This type of instruction, in the same classroom, can be difficult because of the noise level, with two direct lessons occurring at the same time. Teachers tell me that students seem to adjust nicely to the noise, but they have more difficulty adjusting.

## Teach and Monitor

In this approach, one teacher presents the lesson while the other moves around the room, helping and supporting children who need such assistance. As mentioned previously, it is this approach that has created frustration for some reading specialists who feel that they have become nothing more than aides in the classroom. When the reverse occurs and the reading specialist assumes the instructional role, some classroom teachers choose to leave the room or use their "down time" as an opportunity to mark papers, causing concerns in some schools. Nevertheless, there are many opportunities and advantages for such teaming in the classroom. For those working with young children, an extra pair of hands and eyes can be extremely beneficial. For example, reading specialists may teach a lesson requiring first graders to manipulate letter cards as they "build words." The second teacher can be extremely effective in making sure children have the right cards in the right place. Likewise, writing and reading workshops may require monitoring (and conferencing) by both teachers. Another advantage of this approach is that classroom teachers observe the reading specialist using a specific strategy with which they may not be familiar. If the classroom teacher is teaching, the reading specialist can observe students with reading difficulties and note how they behave in a group setting ("kidwatching").

## Team Teaching

Team teaching may include aspects of each of the models described above. In this model, both teachers plan how they will conduct instruction, whether for a particular lesson or over time. The previous scenario of the third-grade teacher and reading specialist described team teaching. Both teachers have specific roles based on their expertise and interests. Each works with the entire group as well as with small groups or individuals within that group. Such teaming requires time for planning, a good working relationship between the two individuals, and common beliefs/ideas about reading instruction and classroom management.

# HELPING STUDENTS SUCCEED
# IN THE CLASSROOM WHILE DEVELOPING
# NEEDED SKILLS AND STRATEGIES

One of the dilemmas faced by reading specialists is that of determining where to put their focus. Should they emphasize helping students succeed in the classroom, or should they help students to achieve those skills/strategies that they are missing, based on assessment results? There is no simple answer. In fact, the only solution is that of doing *both*. Students who are reading below grade level and struggling with the material in their classrooms deserve to receive the help they need so that they can achieve some degree of success. At the same time, these students may benefit from opportunities to work in small groups or individually, so that the reading specialist can review and reteach the specific skills with which these students are having difficulty.

## Focus on Classroom Success

The need for congruence between classroom and reading specialist instruction is recognized as important when working with struggling readers (Allington & Shake, 1986; Walp & Walmsley, 1989). Allington (1986) decries the fact that struggling readers, who are least able to make accommodations, may experience two separate and distinct instructional programs. Reading specialists can promote congruence by reteaching or reviewing a specific skill or strategy important for classroom performance. They can also provide additional practice with specific vocabulary words needed for a selection, guide students in repeated readings of selections, and help with specific assignments.

Although this emphasis is important in the primary grades, it is especially essential for students at upper levels where they are using reading to learn new concepts in various subject areas. What skills and abilities will help the middle school student read and comprehend his or her social studies textbook more effectively? What are the note-taking skills and review strategies that students in a biology class can use so that they are prepared for the unit test? When reading specialists address these areas, they are most likely to prepare instruction that can be used as part of the ongoing procedures in the content classroom. For example, the reading specialist may choose to demonstrate the use of an anticipation guide (Buehl, 2001) with tenth-grade students taking a biology class. Such a lesson highlights for the students the importance of thinking about what they already know and still want to learn before reading a chapter. It also demonstrates for the teacher an approach that can be used to build and activate students' prior knowledge in preparation for reading of text. In this case, the reading specialist works in the classroom with the teacher to promote successful classroom performance.

## Focus on Meeting Specific Needs

Students who have not learned various skills or strategies need to have opportunities to develop them; otherwise, they may always have difficulty with reading. Thus, for students in the intermediate grade who have weak phonic skills, targeting instruction on those skills can be extremely useful. Likewise, if students are assigned textbooks that are above their reading level, they need many opportunities to read silently and orally in books that are at or slightly below their instructional level. The bottom line is that these struggling readers need opportunities to achieve success—and providing instruction at an appropriate level will enable them to experience that. Reading specialists at the secondary level may wish to organize a specific class in which they can work with small groups of students who are struggling with reading. During that class, they can alleviate some of the difficulties the students are facing by providing review and reteaching of specific strategies or skills. For example, such students may benefit greatly from lessons that help them learn various Latin and Greek roots and how to develop vocabulary with such knowledge. Such lessons should, of course, help students see the relationship between what they are learning in this small-group setting and the subjects they are taking. No matter the emphasis of the specialist, students must be helped to see the relevance of what they are learning and how it can help them to read effectively and achieve success in their classrooms.

## PULLOUT OR IN-CLASS INSTRUCTION: IS THAT THE QUESTION?

In a national survey of reading specialists (Bean, Cassidy, et al., 2002), one of the greatest changes that reading specialists observed was the shift from pullout to in-class instruction. As discussed in Chapter 1, this change has occurred for many reasons. This emphasis parallels the inclusion focus of special education, which stresses the importance of providing help to students in their own classrooms. At the same time, the success that has been attributed to various tutoring programs, such as Reading Recovery (Clay, 1985) and the tutoring component of Success for All (Slavin et al., 1996), has led to a proliferation of programs in which students are tutored individually and away from their classrooms. In the following material, we discuss the benefits and limitations of each setting and what is needed if each is to work. Table 2.2 on the next page identifies bridges and barriers of in-class, pullout, and combination models as described by principals, teachers, and reading specialists (Bean et al., 1995). The benefits of these models can be thought about in three ways: What are the advantages for students? What are the advantages for teachers? How does each model improve classroom instruction as a whole?

### In-Class Models

*Benefits*

In-class instruction is much more efficient in that students are not pulled from their classroom, so they lose neither time (for travel to instruction) nor focus (the emphasis is on what is needed in the class-

**TABLE 2.2. Instructional Setting: Identification of Bridges and Barriers**

| Setting | Principals | Reading specialists | Classroom teachers |
|---|---|---|---|
| | | Bridges | |
| In class | • *Provides more opportunities for collaboration, cooperation, and communication.*<br>• Provides less isolation for students. | • *Provides more opportunities for collaboration, cooperation, and communication.*<br>• Could serve more students. | • *Provides more opportunities for collaboration, cooperation, and communication.*<br>• Provides congruence.<br>• Discourages the labeling of children. |
| Pullout | • *Provides students with a place and opportunities to feel special.*<br>• Serves more students. | • *Provides a special environment for young students.*<br>• Requires collaboration and cooperation to be successful.<br>• Provides positive learning experiences in small groups. | • *Provides a comfortable environment in which students can try new strategies.*<br>• Provides opportunities for students to develop positive self-esteem and self-confidence.<br>• Provides special/ individualized attention for students. |
| Combination | • *Provides the flexibility to do what is best for the students.* | • *Provides flexibility of setting when students' needs are better met outside of the classroom.*<br>• Provides flexibility for personality and philosophical differences between specialist and teacher. | • *Provides flexibility to change settings when necessary.*<br>• "Mirrors the need of the people and children involved." |
| | | Barriers | |
| In class | • *A reading specialist acting in the role of an aide.*<br>• Reading specialist permitted to work with Chapter 1 students only. | • *A reading specialist acting in the role of an aide.*<br>• Increases the distractibility of students.<br>• Collaboration, cooperation, and communication are difficult.<br>• Provides little flexibility for personality and philosophical differences between specialist and teacher. | • *A reading specialist acting in the role of an aide.*<br>• Team teaching is difficult.<br>• Encourages a pullout model within the classroom.<br>• Improper scheduling provides no time for cooperative planning. |

(*continued*)

TABLE 2.2. (*continued*)

| Setting | Principals | Reading specialists | Classroom teachers |
|---|---|---|---|
| Pullout | • Reading specialist's room is in an undesirable facility.<br>• Could serve fewer students. | • Teacher penalizes student for going to Chapter—such as making up work during recess. | • Resentment on the part of students for being pulled out—they miss a lot of classwork.<br>• Does not fit integrated approach.<br>• Improper scheduling provides no time for cooperative planning.<br>• Promotes labeling of students. |
| Combination | • None expressed. | • None expressed. | • None expressed. |

*Note. Italicized* text indicates trends across groups. From Bean, Trovato, and Hamilton (1995, p. 211). Copyright 1995 by the College Reading Association. Reprinted by permission.

room). Furthermore, there may be less stigma when students are not pulled from their classrooms; in other words, students are not identified as "different" from others. Additionally, students who are not targeted for assistance also may benefit from the instruction occurring in those classrooms.

When an in-class program is working effectively, teachers often feel that they learn from each other and that the quality of instruction is greater as a result of the sharing of ideas and materials. Some instruction is much more effective with two teachers in the classroom— for example, writing or reading conferences, monitoring work of young children who are using manipulatives. Here, the reading specialist can observe how the targeted students perform in the classroom setting.

Also, the learning that occurs with two teachers can carry over to the entire day and to the entire curriculum. Over time, communication and collaboration between the two teachers occur more naturally, with each having a better understanding of the other's expectations.

### Potential Problems

Given the benefits discussed above, why have in-class programs in some schools languished? As mentioned previously, past traditions and our current model of schooling have not promoted such collaboration and shared teaching. We are much more accustomed to the traditional model in which each teacher is responsible for his or her classroom. As we discuss each of these potential problems, we can consider them in relation to students, teachers, and classroom instruction.

Some students may have difficulty learning in a whole-class setting and may need the privacy and quiet afforded by a pullout model. They may also need more intensive work in a one-to-one setting. Likewise, the in-class setting may not afford opportunities to work on skills/ strategies that particular students need; rather, the focus may be on helping students to achieve in that particular classroom. Moreover, students may still be identified as "different"—especially if *pullout* has simply been changed to *pull aside* or *pull back*!

Probably the greatest difficulty with in-class programs is that of differing and conflicting philosophies of teaching or even classroom management. Some teachers do not appreciate (and cannot tolerate) the noise and activity that an additional teacher brings. Neither teacher may have the knowledge and skills necessary for undertaking such a venture. This problem is especially likely to occur when mandates are issued and teachers and specialists are thrust into such programs without the necessary professional development. There are also concerns that reading specialists are not used appropriately (feel like an aide) or are assigned so many classrooms and students that they cannot work efficiently.

Finally, some classrooms are too small or contain so many students that the specialist cannot work effectively. In some schools, reading specialists lack the space of a working area or even materials that they need to work effectively with students.

## Critical Factors for a Successful In-Class Program

1. Teachers and reading specialists have consistently stressed the importance of scheduling common planning time so that they can implement a successful in-class program. Although some reading specialists and teachers, over time, learn to plan effectively via written communication or "on the fly," these approaches are not as effective as two or more teachers sitting down and planning together.

2. Both the reading specialist and the teacher must be willing to "share" the students. This willingness occurs only when the two have respect for each other and are able to agree on, and enforce, consistent

rules for classroom management and student behavior. The two teachers must also talk openly with each other about their beliefs and instructional practices. Such conversations can lead to successful compromises regarding how the in-class model operates.

## Pullout Programs

### Benefits

One of the benefits of pullout instruction is that students, when pulled, get the specific instruction that they need (e.g., strategies for improving their comprehension skills, word-attack skills) in a small-group or individual setting, where they can focus on what they are learning. There is evidence that individual tutoring (Pikulski, 1994; Wasik & Slavin, 1993) and small-group instruction are beneficial to students (Elbaum, Vaughn, Hughes, & Moody, 2000; Sackor, 2001) and that such instruction, when provided by a well-trained teacher, can improve students' reading achievement. Classroom teachers may feel that they can better focus their instruction to address the needs of the remaining students. Reading specialists can certainly focus their instruction; they do not have to worry about creating a distraction in the classroom; and they have the materials they need to implement their lessons.

### Potential Problems

One of the criticisms of the pullout model is that students lose time as they move from one room to another. One reading specialist commented: "I've had to develop an incentive program to encourage children to arrive at my room on time. It's amazing how they can dawdle as they move through the halls, stopping at the water fountain, the bulletin board, or just wandering along." Another criticism is the stigma that occurs when students must leave their classmates to receive special instruction. At times, classroom teachers have been critical of the pullout model, feeling that students are missing important instruction, or disliking the disruption that occurs when students leave or enter the classroom. The anecdote in Chapter 1 (pp. 3–4) certainly speaks to teacher concerns about pullout programs. Reading specialists too may feel that they are less aware of what is going on in the classroom, both in terms of how specific students perform and how teachers are presenting the literacy curriculum to their students.

### Critical Factors for a Successful Pullout Model

In order for pullout models to work, there must be careful planning and collaboration between the reading specialist and classroom teachers. Reading specialists should be aware of what is occurring in classrooms, even though they are teaching students away from the classroom. One suggestion is that reading specialists spend some time in the classroom, observing students and teacher instruction. This experience provides the reading specialist with a better sense of how his or her students perform and behave when in a large-group or classroom setting. Furthermore, it should be made clear to teachers as to whether or not the instruction received in the pullout setting is supplemental or the core program for students.

In the vignette written by Lucy Klocksin, a reading specialist who works in a large urban elementary school (see pp. 33–37), she describes how she handles her instructional responsibilities. Because of the number of students she serves, she works in a pullout setting. Notice the formal and informal ways by which she communicates with teachers. What is evident is that Lucy is available to work with teachers at various times, including before and after school, given that she does not share a common preparation period with all teachers.

## IDEAS TO FOSTER EFFECTIVE COLLABORATION IN INSTRUCTIONAL ROLES

Regardless of whether the reading specialist works in a pullout setting or goes into the classroom (or both), the following ideas have been helpful to reading specialists in fostering effective collaboration.

1. *Time.* Teachers appreciate the fact that the reading specialist is in their classrooms as scheduled (even if the teachers are not quite ready for them). In talking with teachers about reading specialists, one of their primary complaints was that specialists did not arrive in their classrooms as expected. Arriving and leaving on time are critical, as is adhering to the schedule when taking students from the classroom.

2. *Be prepared!* Have everything needed to teach a lesson, including the magic markers, scissors, dictionaries, books for practice, etc. If going into the classroom, do not assume that the teacher will have the material needed—or be willing or able to take the time to find it. Reading specialists who teach in classrooms have developed ingenious systems for organizing and carting materials, from using luggage with wheels, to movable carts, to milk carton containers.

3. *Discuss and establish responsibility.* It is critical that the reading specialist and classroom teacher decide early in the process who will be responsible for giving grades, writing report cards, and making telephone calls to parents about performance.

4. *Offer to help.* As the reading specialist with special expertise, it is important to think of ways to be helpful in the classroom. Perhaps the teacher is covering a special unit in which students need to take notes—this would be a great time to give a mini-lesson on note taking to the entire class. Or the teacher may be doing the midyear assessments with her students and need some help with students who have been absent.

5. *Meet your commitments.* Teachers have difficulty when reading specialists make changes in their plans, even if there are legitimate reasons for such changes (e.g., need to attend an Instructional Support Team meeting to discuss the needs of a specific student or a meeting requested by the principal). These unforeseeable occasions do happen, but to the degree possible, reading specialists should alert the teacher as soon as possible and make arrangements to reschedule.

6. *Be flexible!* Although the reading specialist may be on time and prepared, teachers and their classes may not be ready or even present. Assemblies, fire drills, health examinations, and many other events compel teachers to change or adjust their plans. These occurrences are, of course, frustrating to the reading specialist but may not be avoidable. *Adjusting* is the only helpful response. If some change needs to be made in the lesson (e.g., the teacher did not complete yesterday's lesson and wants to work with the entire group), the reading specialist can volunteer to assist by helping the students who may have difficulties completing the task or try to rearrange his or her schedule so that the plans can be implemented at a different time. Or it may be a time that the reading specialist returns to his or her office or room to do some additional planning, or an opportunity to assess a child new to the school.

## SUMMARY

Although most reading specialists have instructional responsibilities, the way in which they fulfill them may vary. The key to enacting an effective instructional role is collaboration. Reading specialists must know how to work collaboratively with their colleagues to ensure effective instruction for students. There are many different ways of working collaboratively, some of which are more effective when working in the classroom and others more appropriate in pullout settings. Deciding where to work (in-class or pullout) is not the key question to ask regarding instruction for struggling readers. Rather, reading specialists need to think about and identify their instructional goals and how best to achieve those goals, given the climate and culture of the school and the needs of the students.

### Reflections

1. What do you think are the skills and abilities that reading specialists need if they are to work effectively in the classroom? In pullout settings? Both?
2. What skills and abilities do teachers need to work with reading specialists? In what ways are the skills and abilities needed by reading specialists and teachers the same? Different?
3. What types of lessons would work best with each of the approaches to collaborative teaching?

### Activities

1. Observe a reading specialist in an in-class setting. Write a description of what he or she and the classroom teacher are doing. Which approach to collaborative teaching is used? What are your responses to this approach?
2. Observe a reading specialist teaching students in a pullout setting. Write a description of what he or she is doing with students. (Be sure to ask the specialist how he or she made decisions about the instruction.)

# Lucy: A Reading Specialist in an Urban Elementary School

*Some questions to think about:*

What lessons can be learned about the role of the reading
    specialist from this vignette?

What questions come to mind from reading this vignette?

What key characteristics or behaviors make Lucy an effective
    reading specialist?

My responsibilities as a reading specialist seem to focus almost entirely on
providing services to at-risk students. However, I learned early in my ten-
ure at this job that there is a lot more to it than that. Although working
with struggling readers is the largest and most rewarding part of my job, I
also handle many other responsibilities.

## Working with Volunteers

Since 1,000 students attend my school and I am the only reading specialist,
I have needed to find ways to stretch myself. I trained nine parent volunteers to work with first and second graders who are having trouble learning
to read. It seemed more feasible to train these parents to walk children
through a process each day and expose them to reading than it would be to
train the volunteers to diagnose and help remediate older children's difficulties. Each volunteer sees five students, one-to-one, 5 days per week.
Once trained, each parent is assigned to one classroom and meets with me
weekly to share successes, discuss problems, request materials, and talk
with other parent volunteers. Although this system doesn't allow for our
struggling primary children to receive the services of a reading specialist
directly, it does allow for about 50 students to get one-to-one attention in
reading every day. Since our school is among the poorest funded in the state
(less than $7,000 per pupil, per year) this system is the only possible way
we can afford to provide early intervention services for our youngest children and also address the needs of our older children. We have gotten good
results for 7 years. I see the neediest third–eighth graders myself.

## Instructional Role

The most rewarding part of my job is definitely the teaching part, and, thankfully, I have a lot of autonomy in the way I provide those services. I realize that most experts don't currently consider pullout programs to be the optimum service model. However, in my situation, I feel it is a realistic way to get the job done. When I think about visiting the 17 classrooms from which I pull students, it makes my head spin. I can't imagine being able to create a schedule to serve all these students that would provide the amount of focused reading instruction that I give now.

My groups average four or five students, and I work with 12 groups in all. I meet with each group twice each week for 35–45 minutes. It's not enough time, but it's all I have. I group students by instructional reading level, which means students may not all be in the same grade. Most of the students work hard and make good progress.

Communicating with the 17 teachers from whose classrooms I pull students can be a daunting task, and I always feel I should do more. I made a little form headed "Update from the Reading Resource Room" and had my local printer duplicate it onto paper that automatically makes four carbon copies in different colors. I write up a few sentences for each of my groups, explaining what we are reading, what strategies we are working on, successes of a student or group, or areas of concern. Then the carbons are sent to each teacher. I would like to say that I send these notes each day, but in reality it happens every few weeks. Often those notes open doors for further discussion with teachers, who will see me in the hall after getting a note, and a conversation will ensue.

In addition to these notes, I try to make myself as available as possible. I come to school a little bit early and stay quite late, so that teachers who wish to talk to me about students will have the opportunity. Providing this open space is important because there are many teachers with whom I don't have a common prep period or lunch break. I don't have the opportunity to speak personally to each teacher daily or weekly. Some teachers are always eager to discuss students with me, whereas others aren't, and I probably put more effort into seeking out those teachers who will want to talk about students than the others. Coordination with classroom instruction is difficult when children come from so many classrooms. I try to find out what literature or social studies topics are being studied in each class, and when it is possible, I select material that will increase students' background knowledge on key topics. On rare occasions I have a group of children who all come from one classroom, and in those cases I do try to coordinate my lessons around class work, while still focusing on the reading strategies the students need.

## Assessment

Our school system administers two annual standardized tests to students in most grade levels. One of the tests is a "high-stakes" test, which I use as a screening device. I administer informal reading inventories (IRIs) on about 10% of the school population that performs poorly on the tests. Students who are not in special education, are English language learners, or do poorly on the high-stakes test and an IRI usually receive services from me. I also do IRIs on the students in my program in January and May. Finally, I do IRIs on many of the students who transfer to the school or are being considered for placement in special education. Clearly, this system means I spend a tremendous amount of time administering IRIs, but the diagnostic information gained from these assessments, especially in relation to the time spent, can't be beat.

## Leadership (the Resource Role)

I try to serve as a resource for any teacher or administrator who asks for my input. This is usually a rather informal system, in which I run into a colleague in the hall and he or she asks a question and we figure out a time to talk further, if needed. Teachers ask for my ideas on teaching comprehension strategies, appropriate children's literature, special education referrals for students I see, and a host of other problems. I don't always have the answers to their questions, but I try to help in any way I can. I also work on our annual school improvement planning committee and other committees that deal with literacy issues.

## Challenges

The biggest challenge I face is the limited amount of time I can spend with each group of students. The fragmentation of that time can be frustrating. Every day I wonder if I should serve fewer students and spend more time with them. It's an issue with which I continue to grapple. The fact that I can see kids just 90 minutes per week, or less, can be frustrating. Given that I see about 50 students, I feel I have very little choice, however. That's why connecting with the teachers in the building is a necessity. Helping teachers become more effective reading instructors is another way to stretch myself.

Obviously, finding ways to get the absolute maximum squeezed into every minute is critically important, so another challenge I face is staying organized enough to get everything done. I NEVER speak to another teacher without writing down something that needs to be done. If I don't bother to write things down, I end up dropping the ball sooner or later.

A final challenge that I face concerns the at-risk population I serve. These children have a rate of chronic truancy that is double that of the school as a whole. It's not at all unusual for some of my students to miss an average of 1 day of school per week. Consequently these children spend much of their classroom time playing catch up. The high absentee rate helps to explain why some of these children fell behind in the first place. I feel powerless when it comes to this problem. I grapple with ways to reach parents, but the parents in our school speak many different languages, so even finding someone to translate can be difficult. The standard avenues, such as parent newsletters, are of limited use when most of the parents can't read them.

## Preparation

I feel that I was very well trained to work as a reading specialist. In addition to 7 years as a special education teacher prior to taking this job, I was fortunate to study for my master's degree under nationally acclaimed reading professionals. I was lucky to get the training I did, and it has helped immensely. My willingness to work hard has also helped. I know some teachers view the job of the reading specialist as "cushy," but the fact is that if you want to be effective, you need to be willing to put in long days and take a lot of work home. As is the case with any classroom teaching position, there is no limit to the amount of time I can devote to the job.

I feel it is my responsibility to be learning constantly, so that I can serve as a resource to my colleagues and my students. New ideas, new terminology, new methodologies are emerging all the time, so ongoing professional development is a must. And, as a reading specialist, I need to work with all the other adults in the school, and parents, to get the job done. But then I also get to share in the wonderful feeling of watching many students of different ages grow as they receive positive attention.

## Words of Encouragement

There are so many joys associated with my job, but far and away the best part is seeing the progress my students make. Many of the children I see are in dire straits. Normally they read 2 or more years below grade level. The majority of the students I see make enough reading progress that they are close to or at grade level at the end of a year. This is gratifying and exciting to watch. Most of the children want the help I give them and are cooperative and appreciative. What could be better than that?

Finally, I would like to encourage those who are planning to become reading specialists to consider working in an urban or other school of need. After spending a few years teaching in well-funded suburban schools, my interest in urban schools was piqued by a speaker in one of my graduate classes. She funded classroom libraries and staff development for city schools. She urged us to consider teaching in the city, and I am so happy I did. I have found teaching in the city schools challenging and very rewarding. It can be difficult, but the rewards are great!

LUCY KLOCKSIN, MEd
*Boone School*
*Chicago, Illinois*

# 3

*The Instructional Role*

Initiating, Implementing,
and Evaluating

Chapter 2 provided a broad overview of the instructional role, focusing on the need for collaboration, approaches to collaborative teaching, and the strengths and limitations of two settings for instruction (i.e., in-class and pullout). This chapter explores ideas and issues that reading specialists need to address when they develop or initiate a new approach to instructing struggling readers. When implementing an effective program, reading specialists need to understand (1) the culture of the school, (2) the importance of congruence between their instruction and that of the classroom teacher, and (3) approaches to scheduling that permit effective use of their time. The instructional role of reading specialists at the primary or beginning reading level, intermediate or middle school level, and the high school level is examined, and the need for obtaining feedback or evaluating the instructional program explored.

## STARTING A NEW PROGRAM

In most instances, newly hired reading specialists step into a program that is already developed and accepted by faculty at the school. However, there are situations in which new reading specialists, or those who are working in a school, need to rethink or revise the current program. Reading specialists often ask for suggestions about how to begin a new program; most often they are interested in how they can move from a pullout setting to an in-class program. In this section, I discuss some ideas for those who are faced with such a situation.

### Getting the Evidence

Regardless of the type of program under consideration by the school administration, reading specialists and others associated with the possible change should read the literature and research that will help them substantiate their views. They must also share the literature with the classroom teachers who will be directly affected by the change. The information discussed in Chapter 2 should help reading specialists address the advantages and limitations of pullout and in-class programs in relation to their own school and the needs of the students.

### Sharing the Evidence

As mentioned above, classroom teachers need to be part of the decision-making process. They should have opportunities to read the literature and talk with their colleagues and the reading specialists about how the new program will operate. They should feel free to raise their concerns and make suggestions about how the new program might function more effectively. At this time, scheduling teacher visits to schools to observe such a program might be helpful.

### Getting Started

The best way to start a new program, especially an in-class one, is to begin with those who want to do it. Begin with volunteers! Once other teachers see that the program is an effective one for students, they will feel more comfortable becoming part of the program. In school districts that have mandated changes in the instructional program, moving from pullout to in-class, change is much more difficult. By working with volunteers, the reading specialists and the involved teachers can work out the "bugs," and the program will improve as it is expanded into other classrooms. One of my colleagues who worked with administrators often made the statement, "Make haste slowly."

## Ongoing Staff Development

Classroom teachers and reading specialists should participate in staff development, in which they learn more about how to collaborate and how to work effectively in the classroom. The school district may choose to bring in someone from outside the district who is familiar with the work of reading specialists, or the reading specialist and a classroom teacher could discuss and share the work that they are doing. They may also invite other classroom teachers to observe them as they are working in the classroom. Again, teachers may be asked to read a pertinent article, for example, the article by Ogle and Fogelberg (2001) or Bean (2001), so that they are prepared to discuss the potential of the new program and their role in it.

Again, regardless of whether the specialist is initiating a new program or working in one that has already been implemented, he or she needs to think about the culture of the school and the classrooms, the need for congruence between classroom work and special reading programs, and scheduling that maximizes the use of his or her time. These areas are discussed in the next sections.

## THE CULTURE OF THE SCHOOL AND CLASSROOMS

Because reading specialists generally work with many different teachers in a school, it is essential that they become familiar with the school, its procedures, personnel, and climate. Reading specialists, for example, should have an effective working relationship with the principal, given the key leadership role of that position. How knowledgeable is the principal about reading instruction? How does he or she view the role of the reading specialist? How supportive of that role is he or she? A lack of understanding or agreement between reading specialist and principal regarding the specialist's role can create serious problems. For example, the principal who lacks knowledge about the importance of collaboration may not arrange schedules that promote planning between specialists and classroom teachers.

Likewise, reading specialists should have an understanding of teachers' expectations. Teachers who are not accustomed to an in-class approach may not be receptive to the presence of the reading specialist in their classrooms. Teachers do not always understand how they can or should function when there is another adult in the classroom. Some teachers have difficulty "giving" up their students; they are accustomed to providing all the instruction in the classroom. I am reminded of one teacher who told me how she planned for a specific story (that she loved), including the "costume" she wore to introduce the story and the dramatic entrance that she made! Lacking an understanding of how an in-class model might work, she was distraught to think that some of her students would not have an opportunity to be part of that planned experience. Teachers who are insecure in their role might be threatened by the presence of another professional in the classroom. On the other hand, most teachers, given the staff development needed to learn how to teach collaboratively and the rationale for such instruction, are willing to try the new procedures.

Reading specialists and their teaching partners need to think carefully about the many different issues related to effective collaboration, especially if coteaching in the classroom is planned. Cook and Friend (1995) identify nine different topics that reading specialists and teachers should discuss on a regular basis: instructional beliefs, when and how to plan, parity issues, confidentiality issues, noise levels, classroom routines (instructional and organizational), discipline, feedback, and pet peeves.

---

*Think about This*

What questions would you raise regarding each of these topics? What are your beliefs about each of these?

---

## Congruence or Alignment

As mentioned in the previous chapter, one of the concerns about pullout instruction is the lack of congruence or alignment between the instruction provided by the reading specialist and that provided by the classroom teacher. Such congruence is important for helping students achieve in their own classrooms, which gives them a sense of self-worth and satisfaction (i.e., "I can do it!").

Walp and Walmsley (1989) discuss three types of congruence: philosophical, instructional, and procedural. They indicate that the easiest form of congruence to achieve is *procedural*, whereby teachers decide when and how they are going to work together in the classroom. How many times per week and for how long will the specialist be there? What are the classroom management procedures? Who will do what section of the lesson? How often will the reading specialist meet with classroom teachers? How will they share information about students? *Instructional* congruence is more difficult to achieve, given the need for both teachers to think reflectively about the strategies and skills needed by students, how teachers will present them, and what materials they will use. And, of course, *philosophical* congruence is most difficult. Often, teachers working in the same school have similar goals and objectives for each grade level and therefore are able to compromise or agree to an approach that is best for students. But if each teacher has deep-rooted beliefs about how reading should be taught and these are not congruent, teachers may encounter extreme difficulties working together. For example, an effective classroom teacher who is deeply committed to whole-language instruction and able to implement a reading program, using this set of beliefs, in a manner in which most children in her classroom are successful in learning to read, may have difficulties working with a reading specialist who wants to provide more structure and explicit instruction for struggling readers. Furthermore, in addition to instructional differences, there may be differences of opinion about how students should be disciplined and treated in the classroom. Some of the major problems raised by specialists are those that relate to teachers' low expectations of students with difficulties and the disrespect with which struggling readers are treated. It is difficult for specialists to work in a classroom in which such behavior occurs, given that they have little authority or opportunity to intercede or change behavior.

Walp and Walmsley (1989) make clear that reading specialists and teachers within a school need to discuss the term *congruence* and what it means. They indicate, for example, that congruence may *not* mean "more of the same," nor does a "different" approach necessarily hinder congruence (p. 366). The key to congruence may lie in the philosophical or theoretical approach to reading and to reading disability used by both. By discussing and sharing knowledge about what, how, and why various aspects of reading are being taught, reading specialists and classroom teachers may have a more informed understanding of the instruction in both settings.

---

*Think about This*

What do you think can be done when there are philosophical differences between teacher and specialist in their beliefs about reading or their approaches to classroom management?

---

The answers to this question are not easy or definitive. Sometimes the specialist can make a difference just by serving as a model. The fact that the reading specialist is an advocate for struggling readers may also make a difference. If there is serious concern about how teachers treat students, specialists may need to consult with supervisors regarding what can or should be done. Specialists too must have someone with whom they can share their experiences and problems.

Overall, teachers and specialists alike want to do their best to help students learn; therefore, it is infrequent that specialists find them themselves in unworkable situations. Nevertheless, they should be aware that such a situation can occur.

## Making a Schedule

There is no easy solution to developing an effective schedule. It depends upon the number of students with whom the reading specialist is required to work, the numbers of classrooms in which these students are placed, and the type of program the reading specialist wants or is required to develop. It also depends on the time allotted to the reading specialist for instruction. In some cases, reading specialists are assigned to instruction for every period of the day (except for the usual planning period and lunch). In other schools, reading specialists work with students for part of a day, and the remainder is used for various other activities, such as working with teachers or addressing assessment needs.

In the study of reading specialists in exemplary schools, the numbers of students with whom reading specialists worked varied from 20 to 80, with a mean of 52 (Bean, Swan, & Knaub, 2003). Certainly, the specialist assigned to 20 students can design a schedule that is very different from one responsible for working with 56 students. Issues that need to be addressed include the following:

- How often per week can the reading specialist meet with certain students (should this vary, given the specific ages or difficulties of students)?
- Which students should be worked with in a pullout setting?
- In which classrooms can the reading specialist function effectively (or for what part of the lessons can the reading specialist function within the classroom)?

## WORKING AT VARIOUS LEVELS

In the following section, I describe the work of three reading specialists, each working at different levels. It will become obvious that the roles they fill have many similarities, even though there are also differences in how the specialists schedule their time and where they put their emphases.

### Yvonne: A Reading Specialist in the Primary Grades

Yvonne is a certified Reading Recovery teacher and also serves as a reading specialist for kindergarten and first-grade students in one school in her district. During the afternoon, as part of her Reading Recovery role, she works with four first-grade students who have been identified as needing individualized support. She follows the procedures and strategies required as part of the Reading Recovery program, seeing each student for 30 minutes a day.

In the morning, Yvonne schedules her time so that she can work in the classrooms of the three kindergarten and first-grade teachers (see Figure 3.1). She also meets with each grade-level team once every 2 weeks, during which time she and the teachers discuss (1) the specific skills, strategies, and content that teachers will be presenting, and (2) specific students who are experiencing difficulty and what instruction might help them.

Yvonne works in each of the first-grade classrooms three times a week. On 2 days, she assists the classroom teacher who is presenting an activity-based phonics lesson to the whole class; this activity requires children to manipulate letter cards on their desks. She walks around

| Time | M | T | W | Th | Fri |
|------|---|---|---|----|----|
| 8:30–9:10 | Gr. 1-A | Kdg. A | Gr. 1-A | Kdg. A | Gr. 1-A |
| 9:15–9:55 | Gr. 1-B | Kdg. B | Gr. 1-B | Kdg. B | Gr. 1-B |
| 10:00–10:40 | Gr. 1-C | Kdg. C | Gr. 1-C | Kdg. C | Gr. 1-C |
| 10:45–11:25 | Planning Time ————————————————————▶ | | | | |
| 11:20–12:10 | Lunch | | | | |
| 12:15–3:30 | Reading Recovery/Planning/Preparation Period | | | | |

FIGURE 3.1. Yvonne's schedule.

helping individual students who are having difficulty. In one of the first-grade classrooms, she conducts the lesson so that the teacher, new to the district, can learn the procedure. In this classroom, the teacher monitors the students' work. Often, if there is time after this mini-lesson is completed, Yvonne pulls aside a few students and asks them to read material in which they can practice the skills they are learning. (The other students write their new words in a journal or complete assigned work.) One day, Yvonne works with a small group that needs additional review of the skills taught that week. While she is teaching that group, the teacher is either holding reading conferences or teaching another group that may also need additional help with some strategy or skill. The groups change each week, depending upon the needs of the students.

In the beginning of the year, in the kindergarten, Yvonne and the teachers are focusing on phonemic awareness activities. Either she or the teacher teaches the lesson while the other assists and reinforces the students' work. These lessons last only 15 minutes. Then Yvonne works in one of the centers that has been set up in the classroom, generally helping students who have been identified as needing help with letter recognition or concepts of print. Yvonne also helps when there is a writing activity, taking dictation as students tell her what they want to say.

*Think about This*

What do you see as potential problems in Yvonne's situation?

What do you think are the strengths of this plan for the
   reading specialist?
In what ways is Yvonne supporting the professional growth
   of teachers?

## Greg: A Reading Specialist at the Intermediate Level

Greg works in a setting where the intermediate teachers, grades 4–6,
teach either the language arts block or math, science, and social studies.
His major role is to provide instruction for struggling readers. At the
same time, the principal has asked him to serve as a resource to teachers
and has allowed him to develop a schedule that provides him with that
opportunity (see Figure 3.2). Greg works in the classrooms two times a
week with the six teachers responsible for teaching the language arts
block. This schedule necessitates careful planning so that when he is in
the classroom, he can work productively. During his time in the classroom, he works with a small group needing additional support with vocabulary or comprehension skills. He may also assist by holding conferences with students about their writing. On Fridays, Greg's schedule
allows him to work where needed. He may work with students who
have special needs or with teachers who are addressing a specific issue
or topic (e.g., outlining). He also uses this time to assess students about
whom the teachers are concerned.

| Schedule | M | T | W | Th | F |
|---|---|---|---|---|---|
| Period 1 | Gr. 4-A | Gr. 4-B | Gr. 4-A | Gr. 4-B | float |
| Period 2 | Gr. 5-A | Gr. 5-B | Gr. 5-A | Gr. 5-B | float |
| Period 3 | Gr. 6-A | Gr. 6-B | Gr. 6-A | Gr. 6-B | float |
| Lunch | | | | | |
| Period 5 | Work with math/science/social studies teachers/assessment/ planning with teachers | | | | |
| Period 6 | Same as period 5 | | | | |
| Period 7 | Planning ⟶ | | | | |

FIGURE 3.2. Greg's schedule.

Greg works with the content area teachers to help them teach reading effectively in their areas. He has gone into classrooms to work with students on study skills or conduct mini-lessons requested by the teachers. He did a lesson on writing a research report (how to organize it) for the sixth graders who were given this assignment in social studies. He also did a demonstration lesson, introducing the students and the teacher to the K-W-L strategy (Ogle, 1986) as a means of activating prior knowledge, creating enthusiasm and an organizational framework for the unit on machines and how they work (for the fifth-grade science teacher). At times, Greg schedules planning with the various teachers during his afternoon periods.

*Think about This*

What problems does Greg face with this schedule?
What skills do you think are essential if Greg is to be
    successful in this situation?

## Brenda: A High School Reading Specialist

Brenda is the *only* reading specialist in a large high school, making her job a very difficult one. She has a flexible schedule, except for three periods each day when she teaches small groups of freshmen who scored at a low level on the reading assessment measure given the previous year. Brenda makes arrangements to work with a small number of teachers for a specific unit. She believes that spending more time in a specific classroom (perhaps almost every day while the unit is being taught) gives her the opportunity to become better acquainted with the students and their needs and with the teaching style and goals of the classroom teacher. Thus, during one 4-week period, Brenda team taught with the civics teacher a unit about American democracy. In one lesson, Brenda presented information on note taking, after which the teacher gave a short lecture to the class about the topic of voting rights and responsibilities. Brenda and the teacher then had the students work in small groups to compare their notes and to discuss how note-taking had helped them organize the material. Brenda also did a mini-lesson on taking notes from books. During this same time period, Brenda worked with one other teacher using the same collaborative model.

Brenda's other responsibilities include assessing students at the request of teachers and working informally with teachers who want to talk to her about students or instruction that facilitates their understanding of text material. Brenda also shoulders the major responsibility for making presentations to faculty that address how they might improve their instruction by using various reading strategies. Next month, she will make a short presentation on how teachers might help students write summaries of what they have read. She will also volunteer to demonstrate this strategy in classrooms.

*Think about This*

One of Brenda's difficulties is finding the time to work with all the teachers who have requested her assistance.

What suggestions or recommendations would you make to Brenda?

What skills and abilities do you think Brenda needs in her job?

Henwood, a reading specialist at a high school level, described her role as a collaborative one (Henwood, 2000). Although she works with students, she most frequently works alongside the teacher in planning and implementing lessons. She sees herself as a resource for both teachers and students. Henwood stated empathetically that she does not want colleagues to regard her as an expert giving advice. "Instead, I needed to be considered a partner in improving the learning of all students, one who complemented the teacher's knowledge of content with knowledge of the learning process that I possessed as a reading specialist" (2000, p. 317). Her instructional work is based on the needs of the students as identified by the teachers. She has opportunities to work with many different teachers and students. For example, she describes helping students learn to write a research paper, assisting one teacher who wanted to change her classroom practice from teacher centered to student centered, and helping another teacher convince students that their reading ability could be improved.

## Similarities and Differences in Instructional Roles (K–12)

What should be obvious from the schedules of the reading specialists described above is that all, primary through high school, have some instructional responsibility. All need to know how to work with struggling readers either individually, in small groups, or as a class. And all need to know how to work collaboratively with the classroom teacher to identify student needs regarding what is required in the classroom curriculum and which strategies or skills the students might need to become successful readers.

As we move through the grades, however, there are differences in how reading specialists function. There is much more emphasis on reading to learn in the intermediate and upper grades; therefore, the reading specialist at those levels needs to be extremely knowledgeable not only about how students learn to read but about how students use reading to learn. They must also be comfortable working with content area teachers who are generally experts in their specific field. Frequently, as mentioned by Henwood (2000), reading specialists at the high school level actually serve more in a resource capacity to teachers than in a direct instructional role. The absence of student contact is often a necessity, given that there may be only one reading specialist at that level. Chapters 4, 5, and 6 provide additional information about serving as a resource to teachers.

Indeed, there are many middle schools and high schools in which there are no reading specialists. However, given the national data that indicate that there are still large numbers of adolescents experiencing reading difficulties (International Reading Association, 1999), there is clearly a need for professionals with expertise in teaching reading to work with students and their teachers. The adolescent position statement published by the International Reading Association (1999) recommends that individual students who have difficulty learning how to read be served by reading specialists; services should include the following:

> providing tutorial reading instruction that is part of a comprehensive program connected with subject matter teachers, parents, and the community;
>
> structuring challenging, relevant situations in special reading classes and in subject matter classrooms where students succeed and become self-sufficient learners;
>
> assessing students' reading and writing—and enabling students to assess their own reading and writing—to plan instruction, foster individuals' control of their literacy, and immediately support learners when progress diminishes;
>
> teaching vocabulary, fluency, comprehension, and study strategies tailored to individuals' competencies;

relating literacy practices to life management issues such as exploring careers, examining individuals' roles in society, setting goals, managing time and stress, and resolving conflicts; and

offering reading programs that recognize potentially limiting forces such as work schedules, family responsibilities, and peer pressures. (p. 8)

This list of services should be useful to specialists who are working in middle and high schools as they think about their own job descriptions and how they function in the schools.

In the vignette on pages 54–56, Marlene J. Darwin, a high school reading specialist, describes her role, discussing the fact that it has taken her 7 years to change her position from one of serving primarily as an instructor for students who were experiencing difficulty to one that requires her to handle many different tasks. Although she still works with students, she is also a resource to teachers, helping them to adjust their instruction to meet the needs of students. Compare what Marlene does with the services recommended in the position statement on adolescent literacy developed by the International Reading Association, listed above.

## GETTING FEEDBACK (EVALUATING THE PROGRAM)

It is important for reading specialists to solicit feedback about their work so that they have the information they need to improve. I suggest that reading specialists think of ways to gather feedback from teachers on a regular basis. For example, midway through the year, the reading specialist might ask teachers to complete a simple questionnaire that raises questions important to the successful functioning of the program (see Figure 3.3 for an example). Or the reading specialist might choose to talk with individual teachers about the program. In that case, the questionnaire in Chapter 2 (Figure 2.2) might provide the impetus for such discussion. The specialists may also want to discuss the program with a supervisor or principal and other specialists. Reflecting on what has been successful and what has not is an important process for program improvement.

A more formal evaluation might involve analyzing the impact of the program on the students. At the end of the year, reading specialists can review the achievement data on the students with whom they have

Dear Teacher:

I am interested in getting feedback from you about the program that you and I are implementing. Both of us want to help students learn to read successfully. Therefore, I would appreciate your response to the following questions. If you would feel more comfortable discussing these with me, I would certainly be happy to sit down with you.

1. Have you seen any improvement in the performance of struggling readers in your classroom?

               None               Some           A lot

Please elaborate:

2. Have you seen any improvement in the attitude of struggling readers in your classroom?

               None               Some           A lot

Please elaborate:

3. How easy has it been for you to make a schedule that enables us to work together?

               Easy               Not easy

4. What can be done to make scheduling easier?

5. What has been the most positive part of our working together?

6. What has been the most difficult aspect of program implementation?

7. Any suggestions for program improvement?

Thank you,

_____

Reading Specialist

FIGURE 3.3. Getting feedback from teachers.

worked. How much progress are these students making? Has the program been a successful one for them? If so, in what ways? Chapter 8 provides ideas for assessing student performance.

## SUMMARY

Reading specialists must be able to initiate new programs and work effectively in those that are ongoing. They may be assigned to work in an instructional role at various levels in the schools. Regardless of the level at which they work, specialists need to have an understanding of the culture of the schools to which they are assigned and a good working relationship with the personnel. Likewise, given the need to work collaboratively with teachers, the issue of instructional congruence is an important one; struggling readers need experiences that will help them integrate what they are learning from several teachers. Reading specialists at all levels need to be experts on reading curriculum, instruction, and assessment. Reading specialists at the upper levels need to have an understanding of how students use reading to learn. At all levels, specialists must be able to work collaboratively with other adults. Getting feedback from those with whom they work can provide a basis for program improvement.

### Reflections

At what level would you feel most comfortable working? What qualifications do you have that make you choose that level?

### Activities

1.  Ask a reading specialist to share his or her schedule with you. How similar is that schedule to the ones described in this chapter? What are the specialist's views about his or her schedule (e.g., any problems, why the schedule developed in that way, what is helpful about the schedule, etc.)?
2.  Discuss the following scenario with other reading specialists or classmates. You have been assigned to work with several intermediate grade teachers who teach reading in an in-class program. You have heard other teachers talk about one of them, Frank, as a really tough teacher who makes his students "toe the line." You see yourself as a teacher who "lets

kids have some fun." You give students permission to talk informally and share personal stories, believing that struggling readers need a low-risk environment in which to succeed. You are worried! What do you think you should do? (Remember, there is no right answer in this situation; what might work best as you begin your work with Frank?)

## Marlene: Reading Specialist in a High School

*Some questions to think about:*

What lessons can be learned about the role of the reading specialist from this vignette?

What questions come to mind from reading this vignette?

What key characteristics make Marlene an effective reading specialist?

### The Beginning

Seven years ago, I transferred from a middle school, where I was teaching a reading elective class, to a high school to work as a full-time reading specialist. At that time, all high school reading specialist positions in the county were converted to "discretionary" positions; each principal could chose to maintain or to redesignate the position. Although I had some misgivings about job security and about working with high school students, I applied for the position and was hired as the reading specialist at West Springfield High School.

The journey that I have taken over the ensuing 7 years has been quite simply amazing. Originally I was slated to teach five no-credit classes entitled "Tutorial Learning" (a glorified study hall), to move between five classrooms on a cart loaded with textbooks for every major subject taught at the school, and to be an appendage of the English Department.

At the present time, I teach three credit literacy classes and reasoning skills for SAT verbal prep, lead the West Springfield Reading Initiative, sit on the Reading Council, manage my own work, tasks, and day-to-day activities as a stand-alone department, participate in the instructional leadership team at the high school, coordinate several instructional technology initiatives in the school, analyze data for the administration, teach model lessons in core and elective classes, test students, and provide support in many tangible and intangible ways to faculty, administration, and students alike. The intervening years were filled with many challenges, disappointments, accomplishments, and opportunities to grow as a professional.

## School Profile

West Springfield High School (WSHS) is comprised of students from a middle-class community, most of whom achieve at or above grade level, as evidenced by our scores on various placement examinations and SAT scores. Gradually our population has shifted from 25% minorities to 33% minorities—primarily students from Asian and Middle Eastern backgrounds. Until recent retirements, all the teachers at WSHS had taught there for many years and had well-established routines, procedures, and lessons. Some teachers did not recognize that there were students in their school who had serious, unmet literacy and learning needs. My biggest challenge has been, and still continues to be, bringing those students' needs to the forefront of teachers' minds and into instructional planning.

Compounding the problem, 4 years ago our excellent program was changed to an all-inclusive honors and advanced placement (AP) program, which opened courses at those levels to all students regardless of prior achievement or test scores. Many students who enrolled in these honors and AP classes were not equipped with the requisite literacy skills to be successful in them. My vision was to convince teachers and the administration that my role needed to be expanded beyond teaching no-credit classes to students who needed (but did not necessarily desire) support to teaching credit classes for all students in all classes.

## The Journey

My ongoing quest has been to build rapport with teachers in all departments, as I subtly look for ways to "ply my wares"! Some reading specialists adopt a personal philosophy for their role that aligns them more closely to a classroom model of literacy remediation classes. However, through my own professional experiences and my doctoral course work, I personally adopted a philosophy for my role that moved my influence and knowledge outside the sphere of a remedial class. WSHS enrolls between 2,250 and 2,300 students each year. Within the scope of my remediation classes, I had the potential to impact the literacy and academic growth of no more than 100 students each year, a paltry 4–5% of our total student body. However, if I modeled lessons in classes, I could expand my impact to hundreds of students each year.

I articulated my philosophy and ideas to the administration, offering various examples of lessons and literacy strategies that I could model to teachers and students. Although the administration supported my vision in theory, they were not willing to mandate that faculty participate in these activities or attend any staff development sessions. The principal, however, did give me "carte blanche" to suggest my ideas to teachers, with the caveat that I should not force myself into their classrooms.

Over the years, I have enjoyed considerable success in working with teachers, helping them to discover techniques that would allow them to both teach their content and address the literacy needs of adolescents. Through the support of administration at various levels, the reading specialists of the pyramid (feeder schools) have worked collaboratively to provide staff development for all K–12 teachers under the West Springfield Reading Initiative. This has been a successful endeavor for the teachers as well as the reading specialists.

## Portrait of a High School Reading Specialist

As a secondary reading specialist, I believe that a strong knowledge base in adolescent literacy development, adolescent learning characteristics, sociocultural influences over adolescents, and secondary school culture are imperative. Working with adolescents whose situation seemed hopeless and seeing them graduate makes my efforts worth the difficulties and challenges. Whether I am working with teachers, administrators, students, or parents, the number one skill that continues to serve me well is the ability to believe passionately in the value of literacy and to articulate my beliefs in a nonthreatening manner. In other words, communicating one's vision smoothly and convincingly can foster success for a high school reading specialist.

MARLENE J. DARWIN, PhD
*Reading Specialist*
*West Springfield High School*
*Fairfax County Public Schools*

# 4

## Leadership of the Reading Specialist
### What Does It Mean?

The instructional role of the reading specialist seems to be a given, accepted by administrators, teachers, and reading specialists themselves. Less clear-cut, however, is the leadership role that must be assumed if the reading specialist is to have an impact not only on individual students but on the school as a whole. As mentioned in Chapter 1, the position statement accepted by the board of the International Reading Association (2000) calls for reading specialists to assume a leadership role, suggesting that by doing so, they can exert an influence on the overall reading program in the school. As also indicated previously, in a study of reading specialists in exemplary schools (Bean, Swan, & Knaub, 2003), 100% of the principals in all schools indicated that specialists were important to the success of the reading programs. In addition, in follow-up interviews with a number of the reading specialists, they indicated that they spent much of their time in leadership activities, such as serving as a resource to teachers, conducting professional development, leading curriculum development efforts, and working with other professionals and community members to improve the students' achievement. All but one of the reading specialists interviewed had instructional responsibilities; nevertheless, in varying degrees all were very much involved in leadership activities.

In the position statement of the International Reading Association, leadership is divided into three areas: serving as a resource to others, professional development, and literacy program development and coordination. This chapter discusses qualities and characteristics of effective leadership, working with groups, and serving as a resource to others. Chapter 5 focuses on professional development; Chapter 6, coaching, a specific way of serving as a resource to teachers and providing "job-embedded" professional development; and in Chapter 7, on the development of school reading programs.

## WHAT IS LEADERSHIP?

Given the many different ways in which individuals define leadership, offering yet another definition is not an easy task. Some think of leadership in terms of the role an individual fills, such as the role of principal. Others see it as synonymous with control or influence, suggesting that anyone who can require or influence certain behaviors has leadership qualities. For example, teachers may be influenced by an experienced teacher who is well respected by peers for his or her ability to teach and willingness to state his or her position about various school issues. Others see leadership as a set of behaviors; an individual can assume a leadership role by exhibiting certain behaviors associated with leadership, such as solving problems creatively, obtaining commitments from others, or resolving conflicts. Certainly specific traits or qualifications enhance leadership (e.g., ability to communicate well with others, effective interpersonal skills). Likewise, style (e.g., democratic, laissez faire, authoritative) can influence the way in which one leads.

Leadership in this text is defined as any activities or set of activities associated with working with others to accomplish a common goal: that of improving student reading achievement. This definition is closer to the notion of "shared leadership" described by Lambert (1998). She stated that everyone in the school setting has "the potential and right to work as a leader" (p. 9) and that informal leadership in schools can greatly influence school change efforts. Reading specialists often are expected to lead by influence or by their own personal power (Kaser, Mundry, Stiles, & Loucks-Horsley, 2002).

Often there are situations when reading specialists, knowing the issues and the context, can serve effectively in a leadership role. Say, for example, the school wants to select a new reading textbook. The reading specialist has worked in classrooms with teachers and is well aware of the strengths and limitations of the current textbook. He or she also is familiar with most of the available series, has experience in serving on textbook selection committees, and knows the research on reading instruction. He or she may well be the best person to serve in a leadership role on a committee to select a new textbook. Another reading specialist may take the lead in helping several new teachers who have questions about the most effective ways to use flexible grouping in their classroom. Leaders are those who promote positive change and inspire and empower others to participate in the process. They lead not only by the power of persuasion but the power of example.

## CHARACTERISTICS AND QUALIFICATIONS OF LEADERS

"I think everyone can be a leader. The key is for people to see themselves as being someone who can make a difference."

"One of the important things about leadership is being yourself!"

"True leaders are loyal to those who are under them."

"You have to be reliable. When you tell someone you are going to do something, you need to do it!"

---

*Think about This*

Think of a leader you know and respect. What qualifications or traits does he or she exhibit? What impact does/did that individual have on your behavior?

Do you agree with the four statements above about leadership?

---

The statements above reflect thoughts about characteristics of effective leaders. Just as the definitions of leadership vary, so too do personal views of it, some emphasizing a focus on directing an activity or group, and others seeing it as facilitative behavior. The key is that in schools, everyone—teachers, specialists, and administrators—can serve in a leadership role. When a teacher chairs a committee to select a new textbook, he or she is assuming a leadership role. When reading specialists sit down with a new teacher to discuss how to teach struggling readers in the classroom, they are providing a leadership role. So too when teachers work with a group of volunteer tutors who are coming into the classrooms to assist. The following four qualifications are seen as contributing to effective leadership: ability to communicate, teamwork, empowerment, and goal seeking.

## Communication Skills

### Active Listening

Seek first to understand, then to be understood.
                              —COVEY (1989, p. 235)

Covey (1989), in his book *The 7 Habits of Highly Effective People*, presents this notion as one of the important principles designed to help individuals work with each other effectively. Too often, we listen only half-heartedly because we are busy evaluating, interpreting, or preparing our responses rather than simply trying to understand what the person is trying to communicate. Active listening is one of the key skills of an effective leader. It shows respect and creates trust, without which little may change. The following behaviors contribute to active listening:

1. *Focus on the speaker's message.* Listen to the message for both content and feelings; look for cues that indicate how the speaker feels (e.g., facial expression, body language, posture).
2. *Test your understanding by rephrasing what you heard the speaker say in your own words.* You may also need to ask questions, especially when you are not certain that you have understood the message. Covey suggests that the listener (a) mimic content (i.e., repeat what is said), (b) rephrase content, and (c) rephrase content and reflect feelings (pp. 248–249). In other words, there is a need to *clarify* and *confirm* what we are hearing as well as acknowledge the feelings we are perceiving.

In their book *Joining Together: Group Theory and Group Skills,* Johnson and Johnson (2003) emphasize the importance of nonevaluative listening, indicating that one of the barriers to effective communication is the tendency of individuals to make judgments as they are listening to a speaker. Have you ever found yourself thinking about your reply while another is speaking? Or interrupting a speaker before he or she has finished a sentence? Such behavior is not part of active listening; it not only limits the listener's understanding of the message but can create a negative attitude on the part of the speaker.

## Clear, Congruent Speaking

Johnson and Johnson (2003, p. 140) provide important insights about sending messages. Their list is adapted below.

1. *Own messages by using first-person-singular pronouns.* If you have a particular feeling or opinion about an issue, make certain that you indicate this directly, for example, by saying "I really have problems with ability grouping; these are the reasons."

2. *Make your verbal and nonverbal messages congruent.* Even though you may have a positive message to relate to others, a frown on your face or lack of expression may reduce the impact of that message to others. Listeners attend to more than words: They notice the tone and the nonverbal cues. I had an interesting experience in observing a second-grade teacher recently. Although the lesson was effective, the teacher never smiled or expressed any emotion, even when she complimented certain students on their performance. After the lesson, I asked the teacher whether she still enjoyed teaching (she had taught for many years). Interestingly, she responded, "Oh, yes, I just have a permanent frown on my face. My students understand that I care." In other words, she was well aware of the nonverbal message that she sent, but she also believed that her students saw past her expression to her unexpressed caring. I wonder, however, about the impact of this behavior on students, especially those who were struggling in her classroom. And I was fascinated to discover that she quickly related my question to her facial expressions! (Had others mentioned this to her?)

3. *Ask for feedback about the message.* Taking the time to ask listeners to restate your message or to ask for questions tells you whether you and your listeners are "on the same page" and whether any confusion exists.

*Think about This*

Think about your own communication skills. What do you think are your personal strengths? Possible trouble spots? What communication qualities do you appreciate in others? What would you say to the teacher described above, whose facial expression exhibited a notable lack of enthusiasm?

## Teamwork

None of us is as smart as all of us.
—BLANCHARD, BOWLES,
CAREW, AND PARISE-CAREW (2001, p. 60)

The ability to work as part of a team is an especially important competency for reading specialists, because most frequently the leadership role is one of influence rather than authority. In other words, the reading specialist must be able to motivate others to work together to improve the school reading program. Reading specialists often work with groups or teams of teachers (e.g., committees, grade-level groups). The following standards can be used in shaping effective teamwork:

- The atmosphere is comfortable and relaxed.
- Everyone feels as though he or she has an important role in the group, and everyone participates.
- Group members listen to each other.
- Leadership shifts from individual to individual, depending on experience or expertise.
- The group works effectively as a unit to achieve its tasks.
- Group members are conscious of how the group is functioning (i.e., they are aware of the interpersonal and communication skills between and among group members).

I recommend Johnson and Johnson's (2003) *Joining Together* for those who want to read more about working with groups. They discuss in a clear manner the importance of attending to both *task* and *maintenance* responsibilities of a group. That is, there is a goal to be met, and group members need to work in ways that enable them to focus on that goal. If the group is not staying on task, someone in the group must remind members of their goal; often this is the designated leader. The leader must also be conscious of the importance of maintaining a climate that enhances the members' ability to work comfortably and effectively with each other. Ideas and comments made by members should be received in a receptive manner; all members must be encouraged to participate in the conversation.

## Empowerment

The most effective schools are those in which teachers feel as though they have a voice in what happens; they feel a sense of ownership or empowerment. There are several ways in which leaders can empower others. First, they can recognize the work of others, thus identifying colleagues as leaders. They can also encourage others to actively participate, thus promoting leadership behaviors. For example, the reading specialist may ask an individual teacher to lead a workshop session in which he or she discusses classroom management. In a group setting, the reading specialist as leader may solicit ideas and thoughts of particular group members, especially those who tend to be reticent to speak but who often have great ideas to share. The reading specialist also can provide opportunities for decision making that require group consensus or participation. For example:

> "We've come up with three different ideas about how we want to promote parent involvement in our schools. Let's talk about each of these, what they mean in terms of planning and implementation. I think all of us as a group need to decide whether we will attempt to do all of these or will focus on just one. After listing pros and cons, we should try to come to a consensus as to our future direction."

## Achieving Goals

This final characteristic of effective leadership is what some would call "the bottom line": the ability of the leader to get the job done. When a decision is needed (e.g., about materials or a curriculum issue), the leader must be able to work with others in ways that ensure one is made. First and foremost it is essential to establish (1) a clear understanding of the goal to be achieved and (2) a commitment to achieving that goal. In addition, leaders must make certain that those with whom they are working have the skills and resources they need to achieve those goals. Finally, there must be recognition and support every time a step is taken that moves the group toward goal achievement.

## HOLDING EFFECTIVE MEETINGS

At times, the specialist is the leader of the group, and on other occasions he or she is a member of a working group. In either case, an understanding of basic group dynamics and how to conduct a group meeting is critical for the group to work effectively. General categories of group work are described below.

### Planning

Planning includes setting goals for each meeting, preparing the agenda that assists in meeting these goals, and handling logistics for the meeting itself. It may be productive to spend the first few minutes of a meeting, especially the initial meeting of any group, on helping the group to become acquainted (or reacquainted) with each other. Group leaders may want each member to introduce themselves, share some personal information, or discuss their views about working on the task to which they are assigned. The agenda should be structured so that items of priority are identified first; a specific amount of time can be designated for each item so that those at the bottom of the agenda are also addressed. Part of initial planning includes providing for the place in which the meeting will be held. If the meeting is a large one and information is being presented, a classroom setting with rows of desks may serve as the venue. But if group participation is desired, the room must be one in which participants can sit in a circle and see and hear each other. Often it helps if refreshments are provided, especially if the meeting is an after-school one (a common occurrence). All materials needed for the meeting should be at hand (e.g., handouts, flip charts). Planning also includes making decisions about how records are kept and disseminated.

### Establishing Rules for Group Behavior

The time spent in establishing rules for group behavior is well spent; otherwise, the group may flounder as it attempts to make decisions or handle uncomfortable situations in which individuals are at odds about a specific issue. Rules for the following may need to be addressed:

- What processes for decision making will be used (e.g., consensus, voting)?
- What roles are needed for effective group functioning (e.g., is there a need for a note taker or a facilitator)?
- How will conflict be addressed?
- How will the group make certain that all members have opportunities to be heard?

Although a working group tends to develop its own set of rules and behaviors, the leader plays an important role in helping the group decide upon these and then observe them.

## Attending to Task and Maintenance Aspects

The leader and all group members must work diligently to accomplish their goals or tasks. (Who has not heard grumbling about useless meetings in which items are discussed, rehashed, and then discussed again?) At the same time, the group members must be sensitive to the way in which the group is working so that all members participate, feel valued, and assume a sense of responsibility for group achievement. This is not always easy, and some meetings will be better than others. One of the most effective ways to build a sense of "esprit de corps" is to take time at the end of the session to talk about what went well and how the group might modify its behavior to improve its work.

## Working with Disruptive Group Members

There may be individuals in some groups who are difficult to work with—they do not want to be in the group, they are not accustomed to working with groups, or they antagonize others because they are unwilling to listen to others' ideas. There is no simple answer to working with such individuals. However, there are some techniques that may be effective in dealing with, say, George. First, the leader may want to talk with George privately and describe the behavior about which he or she is concerned, asking, at the conclusion, whether there is anything the leader or the group can do to assist him in working more effectively with the other members. Second, within a group setting, the leader often can reduce the disruptive or hostile behavior by giving George permission to express his frustrations or feelings. For some, having the opportunity to vent reduces or eliminates future negative behavior. Third, setting rules for appropriate group behavior may be the key to changing George's disruptive behavior.

### Planning Again!

A meeting should not end without taking the time to summarize what has been achieved and to make plans for the next meeting. Various members may be asked to take responsibility for handling one or more tasks before the next meeting. Often, it is helpful to send notes or minutes of the meeting to members, highlighting major decisions and reminding members of the tasks that need to be accomplished before the next meeting. And again, taking the time to reflect on what worked well during the meeting provides a starting point for the next meeting.

The ideas presented above are important for reading specialists who have major responsibility for developing school reading programs (Chapter 7). Other books that may be useful to those who frequently work with groups include Johnson and Johnson's (2003) *Joining Together: Group Theory and Group Skills* and Kaser and colleagues' (2002) *Leading Every Day: 124 Actions for Effective Leadership*.

## THE READING SPECIALIST AS LEADER

Each reading specialist will handle leadership responsibilities in a slightly different way, depending upon (1) job descriptions and opportunities, (2) the degree of fit between his or her personality and a leadership role, and (3) his or her leadership skills and abilities. A reading specialist who works with children for six periods a day will have less opportunity to assume leadership roles but can still serve as a leader as he or she works with individual teachers. The new reading specialist, with little experience, may not be ready yet to handle complex or large-scale leadership roles but can work with a mentor to gain experience with such tasks. All reading specialists need to have not only an awareness of their own leadership skills and strengths but an understanding of how to act as an effective leader.

The vignette at the end of this chapter (pp. 75–78) describes the work of a reading specialist who has many leadership responsibilities.

In addition to serving as federal coordinator, she provides professional development for her team of reading specialist interns and for teachers in the building. This responsibility is handled in both formal and informal ways, from meeting with teachers for coffee to scheduling specific times for presentations or workshops. She indicates that the leadership role is the most difficult, but recognizes that her leadership responsibilities most likely have the greatest impact on job effectiveness. When reading the vignette, think about why the leadership role may be the most demanding and most difficult.

Hersey and Blanchard (1977) provide a useful way of thinking about leadership in their discussion of situational leadership. They suggest classifying the actions of leaders into task actions (e.g., achieving the goal) or maintenance actions (e.g., moving the group along in the discussion or taking into consideration the feelings and competency of group members). They purport that various combinations of leadership can be effective, depending upon the make-up of the group: How motivated are members to accomplish this task? How knowledgeable are members? When group members do not have essential knowledge or skills, the leader must engage in high-task behaviors to keep the momentum flowing. Hersey and Blanchard suggest that in these instances, the leader may need to spend more time telling or transmitting information. The leader may also need to convince the members that they can accomplish the job (i.e., selling).

In groups where participants have a great deal of knowledge and are eager to work on the designated task, the leader can work in a different manner, serving as a participant in the group or even delegating responsibility. Imagine the following situation, for example. You are working with a group of experienced teachers who have different views and perspectives about the reading program they are currently using in their school. Their task is to identify criteria that they can use to select new material. All are eager to get new material, but there are some very strong opinions about what constitutes effective reading instruction and agreement is not imminent. Your role (most likely) is to help the group discuss the salient points in an effective manner, remaining sensitive to the different viewpoints and making certain that all members feel as though their thoughts are valued. This group is eager to accomplish the task, and the members have much experiential knowledge. At the same time, they need a leader who can focus them on maintenance or relationship actions that help them to listen, respect different views, and learn from others.

In the following contrived situation, you will need to function differently. In this instance, a third-grade teacher meets with you to tell you that she does not feel that the comprehension instruction she is providing is helping her students. She is interested in learning new approaches to teaching comprehension. This teacher is not confident about what she is doing, but she is willing to seek help. You may need to provide some information about comprehension instruction. Most likely, you do not need to be as concerned about relationship issues as you are in the group work, since this individual has asked for help and wants it. You do not need to convince her that improving her comprehension instruction would be helpful; she knows this!

*Think about This*

How comfortable would you be in your leadership role in the situation with experienced teachers whose task is to select new materials? What difficulties do you foresee in working with this group? What essential skills would you need for working with the third-grade teacher who is seeking information about teaching comprehension?

The following section describes ideas for ways in which the reading specialist can serve as a resource to others. This leadership role is an extremely informal one that can be used by almost every reading specialist, regardless of experience or job description.

## SERVING AS A RESOURCE TO TEACHERS

• *Inform teachers of new ideas and materials.* Such information does not need to be formally presented in a group meeting. Reading specialists can circulate key journal articles to interested teachers and administrators. They can also summarize articles in interesting ways and place them in faculty mailboxes. For example, after reading several articles about fluency, one reading specialist developed an attractive brochure presenting ideas for fluency instruction that could be sent to teachers (see Figure 4.1). When new material arrives at the school, reading specialists can inform teachers that such material is available and volunteer to "try out" the material with a selected group of students.

FLUENCY
The Missing Link
Strategies for Developing Fluency
by
Sandy Akers

Student–Adult Reading

- Adult orally reads story first.
- Student orally rereads story with adult assistance.
- Student orally rereads story as often as it takes to attain fluency.

Partner Reading

- All students listen to teacher read story orally.
- Each student "whisper" reads story to him- or herself. (Teacher assists where needed.)
- Partners reread sentences or paragraphs, switching parts.

Choral Reading

- Students select a short story or poem.
- Students practice reading in unison.
- Students perform their story or play for class.

Reader's Theatre

- Students practice lines from play over and over again until fluent reading is attained.
- Students take their play "on the road" to perform in other rooms.
- Students may add portable props.

Echo Reading

- An adult can read or you can use an audiotaped book.
- Student listens to small passage read by an adult or on tape.
- Student repeats passage using fluent reading and expression.

To learn more about fluency see:

Put Reading First. Washington, DC: Center for the Improvement of Early Reading Achievement (CIERA), 2001.
Rasinski, Timothy V. "Speed does matter in reading." The Reading Teacher, October 2000, pp. 146–151.

FIGURE 4.1. Student brochure. Reprinted by permission of Sandra R. Akers.

Sometimes it is helpful to talk about professional issues at lunch or before or after school. For example, the reading specialist might comment, "So, what do you think about the article in the paper questioning the effect of retention? How does that fit with the policy that we have in our school?"

• *Spread the word about effective teaching and teachers.* Given that reading specialists often observe effective teaching, they can also initiate conversations about what they have seen and encourage visits by other teachers. For example, if one of the second-grade teachers is especially effective in conducting writing workshops, the reading specialist can suggest that another teacher observe in that classroom (with the reading specialist taking over the class of the visiting teacher).

• *Focus on the student.* In my view, most teachers want every child in their classroom to be a successful reader. Often these teachers have tried many different strategies to help various children—sometimes with little success. Therefore, one key approach to serving as a resource to teachers is helping them implement strategies that may improve reading performance of one or more children. During a staff development project in which I served as a resource to teachers in one school, one of the tasks that I most enjoyed was helping a young teacher learn several effective strategies for improving the decoding abilities of her students. We reviewed test scores and discussed several strategies, including Cunningham and Hall's Making Words technique (1994). I then agreed to do a demonstration lesson of that procedure. I also gave the teacher a copy of the book, *Making Words.* The teacher was very excited about the approach and invited me to observe her as she taught. The children were now learning a great deal—and she was excited about their success—and her own.

• *Be available and follow through on your commitments.* Unless reading specialists are "seen" in the schools, there may be little chance of serving as a leader. It is easy to find tasks to attend to, such as paperwork or administrative duties, that take specialists away from the schools. When reading specialists take the time to stop in and visit teachers, post the days on which they will be at a specific school (if they travel), and volunteer to help teachers if they see an opening, they are acting as leaders. Equally important is providing follow-through on every commitment made. Usually, teachers do not understand or appreciate cancellations even when they appear to be unavoidable, for example, the principal may request that the reading specialist attend an important meeting. Certainly, there are times when the reading special-ist may need to cancel or make changes in his or her schedule, but then every effort must be made to ensure the teacher that the commitment will be honored. The teachers should also be informed as soon as possi-ble if there is to be a change in the schedule. Furthermore, the specialist and teacher should collaborate so that rescheduling will occur as soon as possible. Nothing destroys the credibility of the reading specialist more than the lack of follow-through. Teachers soon decide that there is little they can expect from the reading specialist and will close the door, literally and figuratively, to future interactions.

• *Be flexible.* Flexibility is an especially critical quality, because of-ten creative and effective ideas emerge in the moment, as the reading specialist works with a specific teacher or teachers, and their implemen-tation usually requires "on the spot" adjustments to planned work. These ideas may come from the reading specialist or the teacher. The most effective reading specialists quickly think of ways that they can facilitate the development and implementation of these ideas, rather than thinking of reasons why such ideas are impractical. In discussing leadership, Colin Powell said, "You don't know what you can get away with until you try" (in Harari, 2002, p. 65). In other words, reading specialists are most effective when they look for ways to make things work.

Flexibility is also important in terms of working with individual teachers. For example, the reading specialist may be able to work as a coteacher in the classroom to implement guided reading with one teacher, because he or she is especially open to having another adult in the classroom. With another teacher, the reading specialist may only provide material and suggestions about guided reading, giving that indi-vidual an opportunity to think about the approach and how it might be implemented.

## RESOURCE FOR ALLIED PROFESSIONALS

The reading specialist should work collaboratively with other profes-sionals in the building or district. These include the special education teachers, speech teachers, counselors, and psychologists, but may also include teachers of the arts, physical education instructors, as well as others. Reading specialists, special education teachers, speech teachers, and counselors may all be involved with the same students. Therefore, it is important that communication occur among *all* of these professionals. Although many schools have implemented special groups, such as instructional support teams, in which key educators meet together to discuss specific children with special needs, there should also be informal conversations among these educators. Too often, children with special needs receive multiple and possibly conflicting intervention strategies because of the lack of communication among the educators involved with them. Educators can learn about the various approaches that may be used to improve reading performance from one another. For example, speech teachers are often well prepared to teach phonemic awareness to young children, and with the reading specialists' assistance, may be able to work with more teachers or children. Likewise, special educators may appreciate information about the various approaches to teaching reading that the reading specialist can share with them. Special educators, in turn, often have well-designed behavior management programs that they can share with others.

In addition to working with educators connected with children who have special needs, involvement with others, such as the art teachers, librarians, and so on, can promote improvement of reading for all students in the schools. I have observed music teachers whose programs can certainly help young children develop excellent phonemic awareness skills. The arts program can be used in upper grades as a means of expanding and enhancing students' thematic learning in the various content areas. The librarian, of course, can be a source of information about book availability and work with teachers to promote student reading.

Interactions with school psychologists may also be an important part of the reading specialists' role, not only to obtain test information about students but to learn more about the child and to share information that may assist the psychologist in getting a more complete picture of a specific student. Often, the type of assessments that reading specialists administer help psychologists gain a more specific understanding of the child's instructional needs in relation to literacy. Hoffman and Jenkins (2002) conducted interviews with a group of reading specialists to learn more about their interactions with school psychologists. They found that these reading specialists had some collaborative experiences with the school psychologists, but that scheduling time for interactions was a problem. They also talked about the importance of establishing good personal relationships and knowing more about how to collaborate effectively.

## RESOURCE FOR ADMINISTRATORS

Although many principals, especially those in the elementary school, have an in-depth understanding of reading instruction, some do not; given their multiple responsibilities, many do not have adequate time to devote to the leadership of the reading program. They may rely on the reading specialist in their school for specific information about how the school as a whole is doing (e.g., the scores in the various areas of reading: decoding, comprehension, etc.). Principals may also need to be informed as to whether there is a need for additional staff development in the area of reading for specific teachers (e.g., content area teachers in the high school want to know more about how to handle the reading of texts). Reading specialists need to be available to the principal, and as important, to inform the principal about what (1) they are doing in the school, and (2) how the principal can be helpful to them in improving classroom reading instruction.

## SUMMARY

Reading specialists all have leadership responsibilities, but these differ depending upon job opportunities, experience, and the technical skills of the specialist. Such skills include having the ability to (1) communicate with others, (2) work with teams, (3) achieve goals, and (4) empower others. The leadership role for reading specialists is often one that requires leading by influence and that will differ, depending upon the various situations. All reading specialists need to serve as a resource for teachers, administrators, and other professionals involved with struggling readers.

## Reflections

1. Why is the leadership role of the reading specialist an important one? Why is it one of the most difficult tasks of the reading specialist?
2. Think about a group with which you have been involved recently. What

was the style of the leader? How did the leader help the group to work effectively?

## Activities

1. Interview a reading specialist to determine what leadership roles he or she assumes. Ask the specialist to identify what skills are needed to perform such tasks.
2. Attend a group meeting. Think about the leadership style of the leader. How did the group achieve its goals? In what ways did the group exhibit its ability to work together as a team?
3. Discuss the following scenario. What leadership style would be most effective, given the characteristics of the group members?

   A new first-grade teacher has told you that she is having no difficulties teaching her students, is enjoying her experience, and does not need any specific help from you, the reading specialist. However, you have been in her classroom and have noticed some classroom practices that indicate that she has very little knowledge of how to teach phonics.

# Toni: The Job of One Reading Specialist (a Brain on Overload)

*Some questions to think about:*

What lessons can be learned about the role of the reading specialist from this vignette?

What questions come to mind while reading this vignette?

What characteristics or behaviors make Toni an effective reading specialist?

It's Sunday night—time to get back into the "school mode." As I look at my planner, I see another busy week ahead of me. (*What meetings do I have this week? Meetings with classroom teachers? Parents? Administrators? What do I need to prepare for each meeting—handouts, subs to arrange, availability of meeting rooms, e-mails to participants? I need to check with teachers regarding the students about whom we are seriously concerned—also make sure to let the principal know of the concerns. How are my students doing? Have they been reading nightly? Do I need to call home?*)

I am a reading specialist in a small suburban district, Allegheny Valley School District, outside of Pittsburgh, Pennsylvania. Allegheny Valley has a student population of approximately 1,300 students K–12, with a poverty rate of about 28%. I teach Reading Recovery for half of each day, coordinate the federal programs, and am involved in the overall district reading program. In this position I work with classroom teachers, parents, and administrators, and I supervise reading specialist interns from the University of Pittsburgh. The interns are certified teachers, working on their reading specialist certification at the university, taking classes in the evening and working during the day at school districts. It is my responsibility to supervise between three and five interns per year.

(*I love the intern program—such hard working, caring, and competent teachers participate in it—but it is tough to have a total staff turnover each year. I know that the children, the classroom teachers, and the interns benefit from this program, so the work is worth it. This year, the interns are wonderful—wonder what next year will bring? The reading staff is based in the Reading Room—a regular classroom with desks for myself, the three interns, another reading specialist, and a desk for the ELL teacher—six females and lots of materials all in one room. It works for us, and the daily interaction is great. What questions will the interns have for me today? I have to stay on top of things to answer their questions.)*

I love my job—it presents opportunities and rewards on a daily basis. What is it exactly that I do? As I think about my major responsibilities, they fall into three broad categories: assessment, instruction, and leadership. I address each of these areas briefly.


## Assessment

One of my responsibilities is that of overseeing reading assessments given to all of the students K–8. We use the Developmental Reading Assessment (DRA), and my first job was to train all of the teachers in its administration. *(Make schedules for teacher training—cover classes, give teachers time to observe the administration of the DRA and time to practice giving it with support. Are all of the papers copied and accessible to the teachers? Do they all understand how to document errors and record student performance? I hope so, but I'll check as the assessments come in.)* This assessment is given at the beginning, middle, and end of the school year. Each time, the results are used for different purposes. At the beginning of the year, assessment data are used to assist teachers in providing appropriate instruction to the students in their classes. Student reading levels are determined, and books that coordinate with those levels are provided for both independent and instructional purposes. *(I can't believe how well Susie is doing—she read a lot over the summer and her reading really improved. Unfortunately, Jane did not read at all—her reading performance really dropped—need to alert teacher and parents about this.)* Once reading assessments are complete—data entered into the computer, results analyzed, and Title 1 students identified—then parent permission letters are distributed. *(Some parents refuse Title service. Why would they refuse help for their child? It's hard to see a child struggle and not receive extra support.)* Finally, the making of the schedule. *(Scheduling is so hard—there's just no way to keep everyone happy. Why is it that some teachers are so flexible and willing to work with me on this and others are not? Just have to do the best I can—keep the children at the center of all of this—what is best for them.)*

Now that children are assessed, identified, and a schedule formulated, instruction can begin! *(This is the part I love—actually working with the children.)* We work with children using several different models. We go into the classrooms and work with the teachers during the language arts block. We give each teacher 30 minutes, 4 days a week of inclusion time. (*Some teachers use this time so productively, and others wish we weren't in that room with them. They feel we inhibit their ability to be flexible because they are obligated to a particular time block for reading support.*) We also have pullout time with focus groups, when we work with children on their identified areas of difficulty. We also work with some children individually. (*Hard to find pullout time—can't pull out of math, special subjects, recess, or special programs. Teachers want the children to receive this extra help, but they don't want to have to make up the work with them. Please don't punish these children by giving them extra homework because they were out with us.*) As I said, we work with the children 4 days a week, Monday through Thursday. On Friday we work in the Reading Room. (*Fridays are super busy. I have all my plans to get done, meet with the interns to "debrief" about the week, provide some staff development for the interns, usually have meetings to attend. It's great to have the time to get prepared for the upcoming week.*)

## Leadership

Although assessment and instruction are important components of my job, the leadership component (which I find to be the most difficult) has the greatest impact on overall job effectiveness. Numerous leadership issues arise (*particularly those that require interpersonal skills*) in the process of dealing with various groups of people—interns, classroom teachers, parents, administrators, and even school board members. Each participant in the education process plays a unique and important role in the development of lifelong learners. One piece of this process is professional development, which I provide to staff both informally and formally during staff development classes held at our district after school and during the summer. (*The teachers' room is a great place for a short, informal conversation, but be careful—don't let the conversation get too long and totally interrupt the time teachers have to "unwind." Sometimes a brief comment in the hall or a more defined time during a prep period is used to check on students, materials, or other reading-related issues.*) Parent interactions can be informal (*a chat in the hall, a quick phone call or note*) or more formal during evening parent meetings. Keeping administrators informed regarding reading issues and options is yet another audience to educate. Administrators can provide the environment necessary for change. Administrative support I've received has been a major advantage. (*What can I bring to them as another option to improve and extend the reading program in place at the district? They have always been supportive and open if I have done my homework and bring them the information they need to make a decision. I'm really lucky that I've had so much support.)* The leadership role is definitely the most challenging part of the job for me—dealing with so many audiences in effective and productive ways is tough.

## What Can I Suggest to Others?

An important part of my job is staying current in the field. *(This is necessary personally and professionally. How can I ask for change if I don't know what is out there to change to?)* The district facilitates this aspect by sending me to a variety of conferences, some local, some not. The local resource center provides day "classes" in reading-related topics that I attend either by myself or with a team of teachers. I have been to the International Reading Association conference for the past four years. *(WOW—what a way to get rejuvenated—just to talk to and hear so many individuals in the field of reading is so motivating.)* I've also attended state reading and federal programs conferences *(need to know what is going on in the state and locally!)*. Memberships in professional organizations and reading professional journals and books also help me to stay current. *(Wish I had more time to just sit and read—summer is a great time to catch up. I skim lots of material—and mark articles that I want to go back to and read in depth.)*

One thing I can say with *no* reservations: My job is never boring, never the same 2 days in a row, and it has infinite opportunities, challenges, and rewards. Nothing is a satisfying as watching a child evolve into a reader. I love the field of reading and know that it is a complex skill that is crucial for children to acquire in order to function in the world. I have the best job in the world.

ANTONETTE SAUL, EdD
*Reading Specialist and Federal Coordinator*
*Allegheny School District*

# 5

## Professional Development

Given the emphasis on high-quality literacy teaching in every classroom, reading specialists often have responsibilities related to professional development. Professional development can be defined as efforts related to improving the capabilities and performances of educators. Although individuals may seek to improve their own skills through reading, attending courses or workshops, or receiving advanced degrees, much professional development occurs in schools with groups of teachers. Such work can be extremely productive in that larger numbers of teachers are reached, and they can be influenced by their interactions with others in their own buildings. The effort can be site specific and based on goals of the school or district.

In Chapter 4, I discussed leadership skills and abilities, providing information about working effectively with groups. That knowledge is critical for reading specialists involved in professional development efforts. In this chapter, I focus more specifically on professional development, its value, and the components that are essential if it is to have an impact on teachers. I also share data from a large scale professional development project to provide an example of an intensive, long-term, systematic initiative. I conclude the chapter by discussing criteria for making effective presentations—often a requirement of those involved in professional development activities.

## REVITALIZING THE WASTELAND

Concerns about and interest in reading instruction, from national to local levels, have led to calls for improving teacher knowledge and performance in teaching literacy. Moreover, we now have evidence that teacher quality matters. For example, studies such as those conducted by Sanders and Horn (1994) and Sanders and Rivers (1996), which used value-added student achievement data, found that student achievement gains were much more influenced by a student's teacher than other factors such as class size and composition.

According to Snow and colleagues (1998), teachers need support and guidance throughout their careers in order to maintain and update their knowledge and instructional skills. As Louisa Moats puts it, *Teaching Reading IS Rocket Science* (1999). In that publication, the writers indicate that teachers must be experts in order to teach reading effectively. They must know a lot about their subject matter and the instructional strategies that will enable them to provide the best literacy experiences for their students.

Yet professional development, as it has been conducted in schools, has generally been considered the wasteland of education (Little, 1993). Teachers have been introduced to, and sometimes bombarded with, information about new projects or activities that happen to be in fashion at a specific time, often before there is research evidence to establish the innovation as effective. At times, initiatives have been placed in schools without attention to the implementation process. Fullan (1991) talked about the "implementation dip"—the initial difficulty with implementation—indicating that if teachers are not given support, new ideas soon disappear because they do not become part of teachers' repertoire of instruction. Joyce and Showers (1995) called for creating change in schools using a professional development system that is "far more powerful and pervasive than the one that exists" (p. 5).

## WHAT IS PROFESSIONAL DEVELOPMENT?

Guskey (2000) defines professional development as "those processes and activities designed to enhance the professional knowledge, skills, and attitudes of educators so that they might, in turn, improve the learning of students" (p. 16). This definition puts the focus on the end result of such initiatives: improving the learning of students. When professional development is considered in that light, it is much easier to think about how to structure it and how to evaluate it. Such a definition also reflects the belief that there are many different models of professional development, each with its advantages and shortcomings. Guskey identifies seven different models: training, observation/assessment, involvement in a development/improvement process, study groups, inquiry/action research, individually guided activities, and mentoring. Some of these models are more effective than others in specific contexts. Often a professional development plan is based on a combination of models. For example, in a professional development initiative that I codirected, teachers attended workshop sessions throughout the year and were asked to develop a focus or action research project, based upon the needs of their students. Teachers also administered informal assessment tasks to determine the literacy strengths and needs of their students. Furthermore, they were observed implementing various strategies and given feedback about their instruction. In this project, a coach was responsible for helping the teacher understand the various strategies, and he or she assisted in implementation efforts.

In addition to various models of professional development, there are also different levels of professional development, from those initiated at a district level to those that are site or school based, sometimes with only a small number of teachers involved. A district, for example, may decide it will use *Success for All* (Slavin et al., 1996) in all its schools, and thus every faculty member will participate in the professional development training for that program. In this case, the initiative is one developed by "outside experts."

In other instances, district personnel may develop a literacy program based on standards that they themselves have developed or adopted and then provide the necessary staff development (perhaps using both inside and outside experts). These initiatives, whether "homegrown" or based on an outside model, have the advantage of focus, given that all teachers are trained to use the teaching approaches.

Initiatives in which selected teachers volunteer to participate in a specific program are benefited by participants who are excited by what they have decided to do. On the other hand, such initiatives are likely to spawn several problems. The district or school may not completely understand what these teachers are doing; there may be multiple initiatives, and this very plurality may cause problems for teachers and for the school as a whole. In some cases volunteers are not certain of what they have agreed to do!

Individual teachers can attend various workshops or conferences and read journals or books that help them make changes in their instructional practices. These individuals, as described by Joyce and Showers (1995), are the "gourmet omnivores," the 10% of teachers who are always seeking to improve. These teachers are always looking for ways to do a better job of teaching students. Still, they may have a difficult time using these newly learned approaches, which may be different from those recommended or required for use in the school, and the teachers may get little or no support for what they are doing.

---

*Think about This*

What type of professional development have you participated in—school mandated, volunteer group, or individual effort? Discuss your experiences with each.

---

## IMPROVING PROFESSIONAL DEVELOPMENT

What can be learned from the past that will improve professional development for teachers? The standards of the National Staff Development Council (2001) call for attention to content, context, and process issues. Those responsible for professional development must be certain that they have selected the appropriate content for teachers to learn for a particular context. In addition, they must develop and implement processes that recognize the nature of adult learning. The National Staff Development Council standards also call for building the capacity of teachers to use research-based teaching strategies that are appropriate for their students. A discussion of the standards regarding literacy follows.

### Content

What do teachers need to know and be able to do? Reading specialists responsible for professional development have multiple resources that they can access to address this question. The following resources address reading instruction from birth through adulthood and should be helpful to those responsible for planning professional development.

Learning to Read and Write: Developmentally Appropriate Practices for Young Children, 1998. (International Reading Association: *http://www.reading.org* or NAEYC: *http://www.naeyc.org/resources*)

National Center on Education and the Economy (NCEE). Reading and Writing Grade by Grade: Primary Literacy Standards for Kindergarten through Third Grade. (*http://www.ncee.org*)

National Center on Education and the Economy (NCEE). Speaking and Listening for Preschool through Third Grade. (*http://www.ncee.org*)

National Council of Teachers of English (NCTE) and the International Reading Association (IRA). Standards for the English Language Arts. (*http://www.ncte.org/standards*)

Starting Out Right: A Guide to Promoting Students' Reading Success, 1999. (*http://www.nap.edu*)

Learning First Alliance. Every Child Reading: A Professional Development Guide. Baltimore, MD: Author, 2000. (*www.learningfirst.org/readingguide.html*)

Adolescent Literacy Position Statement, International Reading Association.

Standards for English Language Arts: NCTE-IRA. (*www.ira.org/positions*)

In most cases, the identified resources are based on research about literacy instruction; some of them use the evidence presented in the work of the National Institute of Child Health and Human Development (2000) and National Reading Research Commission (Snow et al., 1998).

Reading specialists involved in professional development efforts should, of course, consult the standards developed and often mandated by their state department of education or local districts. They should work with teachers so that there is a common agreement as to what students should be learning at each grade level.

## Context

The creation of a successful professional development plan must be based on the context in which it is to be presented. Several questions must be addressed:

What are the experiences, skills, and abilities of the teachers who will implement the plan?

Is the culture in the school one that is receptive and eager to change?

What are teachers' attitudes about change?

What are the characteristics and needs of the students in this context?

What resources are available from the administration and the community?

In one school, faculty may be quite receptive to new ideas and ready to make changes in how they teach literacy. In other schools, much more preliminary work may be needed before the actual program can be implemented. Often it is necessary for the staff development team to think about current practices and what may need to be eliminated before new practices can be instituted. One of the common complaints of teachers—and rightly so—is that they are always asked to add to what they are doing—in an already filled day!

Other legitimate issues include concerns about various practices that do not seem to fit together, and the lack of support or resources at the school level for a district-mandated practice policy. These issues need to be discussed by key personnel and teachers if the professional development effort is to be successful.

## Processes

*Process* often gets short shrift as teachers receive what some call "drive-by efforts," or as Little (1993) described it, the flavor-of-the-month emphasis. Successful efforts at professional development that generate teacher change have several process-related characteristics in common:

1. *Duration.* Effective programs are long-term or sustained endeavors. They may begin with a workshop in which teachers learn various strategies, but the program continues throughout the year, with opportunities for teacher practice, inquiry, and reflection.

2. *Opportunities for feedback.* Teachers have opportunities to talk about what they are implementing, what works, and questions/concerns they have about implementation. The development plan includes a built-in mechanism to help teachers as they implement the new strategies: Individuals with expertise visit teachers and help them by demonstrating or observing practices and then taking the time to discuss aspects of the work. Such coaching is supportive rather than evaluative. (Coaching as a professional development tool is discussed in Chapter 6.)

3. *Embedded into the classroom practices of teachers.* When the professional development effort is one that is closely related to what teach-

ers do every day in teaching and assessing students, there is a much better chance that the initiative will succeed. One of the ways that this "fit" can be accomplished is to have teachers who have been able to implement a particular strategy effectively present their work to other teachers. Teachers appreciate hearing from those who have actively been able to "do it" in their classrooms, and they value seeing these teachers in action.

4. *Sense of recognition.* Teachers must be acknowledged for the work they do. There must be recognition of those who have "expertise"; for example, such teachers can demonstrate for others or assist others in implementation. My own work with professional development has led me to believe that when teachers feel a sense of accomplishment and empowerment, they contribute significantly to the success of the initiative. They make creative and specific suggestions for how the initiative can work more effectively, and they encourage other teachers to use the new strategies. In LEADERS, a staff development project described below, teachers did much more than expected. They began to think about themselves as professionals, writing for mini-grants, collaborating with others, and thinking about how they might attend and then present at various professional meetings. Some decided to pursue additional graduate study.

## LEADERS: A PROFESSIONAL DEVELOPMENT INITIATIVE

In the following section, the LEADERS professional development project is described as a means of providing examples for each of the elements discussed above (i.e., content, context, and process) (Bean, Swan, & Morris, 2003).

LEADERS (Literacy Educators Assessing and Developing Early Reading Success) was developed and funded by Eisenhower funds for a 3-year period. The initiative was intended to improve the teaching of K–3 teachers in schools where there was low student achievement and large numbers of high-poverty students. In this initiative, the leadership team was university based and volunteer teachers were recruited from various districts that were eligible for the program. One of the first decisions to make was what it was we wanted students to know and be able to do, regardless of the school they attended. We needed to make certain that what we presented was appropriate despite the use of different basals and different curricular efforts in the various districts. In the first year, *Every Child a Reader: Applying Reading Research in the Classroom* (Center for the Improvement of Early Reading Achievement, 1998) was used as a text for teachers. By the third year, the National Reading Panel Report had been published, and each teacher was given a copy of *Put Reading First* (Armbruster & Osborn, 2001).

We believed that the focus should include (1) efforts to increase knowledge and understanding of teachers (i.e., what did they need to know about teaching reading?), and (2) presentations of various strategies or approaches that have been found to be effective in teaching reading. The belief was that regardless of the different basals or anthologies used in schools, teachers overall would find the knowledge and accompanying strategies to be useful in their classrooms.

In order to adapt to the various contexts in which we worked, a site liaison or coach was assigned to each school. This individual had to meet with the principal or superintendent and with teachers to make the necessary adjustments in relation to the school. For example, one school district was subject to a district-wide initiative, and teachers were required to use specific approaches mandated by that district (e.g., a word-building strategy to help students learn phonics; Beck & Hamilton, 1996). We were able to help teachers understand how to use that approach effectively and also share with them specific management strategies that would make their implementation easier. In one school, teachers were asked to "level" their books. The coach for that school worked with teachers at the site to assist them in the actual work of identifying levels for each of the books. In most cases, we were able to adjust or add to our work to meet the needs of a specific school. In one instance, we did experience difficulty because the classroom management system promoted by the district was antithetical to what we were promoting.

The strengths of this professional development initiative lay in the processes we used. The coach (already mentioned) went to the school on a regular basis to support and reinforce the teachers' work by providing demonstrations, observing, and giving feedback, and assisting in the work being done by the teacher (e.g., helping with the administration of the assessment battery to students in each classroom). Working with individual students provided coaches with insights about the teacher's students and helped them develop relationships with the children as well as the teacher. The work done with the children and the demonstration lessons also helped coaches to establish credibility. Each coach functioned somewhat differently (depending on the site). I not only observed, demonstrated, and assisted with testing, I also took teachers to visit another school, attended several parent meetings in the evening, and met with the principals and superintendent to discuss the relationship of LEADERS with other initiatives in the district. One of my colleagues joined a study group of teachers at a school, and they have continued to meet on a regular basis.

Another critical aspect of the project was LAB (Literacy Assessment Battery). We believed that if teachers would use data not only from their observations but also from these informal measures, they would begin to make instructional decisions that would benefit students. Each coach spent time talking with teachers about test results, examining student work, comparing students' work samples, and then discussing what instructional decisions needed to be made.

A third dimension of the project was the "focus" or "action research" project. This project would be based on the results of the LAB. Teachers were asked to decide where they wanted to focus their energies, given the profile of their students. Teachers were required to develop a poster for an end-of-the-year celebration that included examples of the activities they were implementing, displays of student progress, and a statement of what they themselves had learned. Several teachers in one district, for example, recognized the need to improve the writing performance of their students and embarked upon a year-long writing project. They expressed their excitement when they saw their students' enthusiasm for writing in journals and participating in the writing workshop—and when they saw the progress of their students at the end of the year!

A fourth aspect of LEADERS was the opportunity for networking. Teachers indicated that they valued opportunities to talk with others who taught at the same grade level or in other schools or districts. As in most schools, there is very little or no opportunity for teachers to talk with each other during the school day.

As mentioned above, our major focus was enhancing student performance. In what ways did LEADERS affect students' literacy growth? Evaluation efforts from LAB indicated that students made significant progress in each of the assessed components of reading (Bean, Swan, & Morris, 2003). We also were required to assess the growth of teachers on a teacher knowledge test and, again, there was significant growth on this instrument. Teacher satisfaction was also high, as measured by various questionnaires and reports given in focus group meetings. Some of the comments made in the focus group session include the following:

"LEADERS has made the biggest difference in my teaching life. It has worked on empowering teachers—and I thank you for that. I now know how to teach reading. I didn't *really* know what I could do when kids weren't successful with the basal."

"I'm really excited about the assessments. Now I can see what my students need—and work on it."

"I love the coach—it's like having a personal trainer—I'll really miss him next year!"

Schools have chosen to continue with the program, and we have been able to provide the training to all the primary teachers in each school. Some of these teachers returned the following year to make presentations to the new cohort group of LEADERS. Participants really enjoy listening to their colleagues talk about what they have done in their classrooms. Teachers have written for mini-grants and are continuing their efforts to implement the approaches and strategies learned in LEADERS. In addition, they are writing proposals to present at local and state conferences.

Assessment results of students indicate that they too have benefited from the program. Test scores indicate significant gains from fall to spring on all dimensions of reading and writing. Moreover, the improvement in student scores was related to the emphasis or focus of the classroom teacher.

*Think about This*

Think about the initiative described above. What do you see as the strengths of the initiative? What problems or difficulties might be faced by the providers if it were implemented in your school?

## GUIDELINES FOR DEVELOPING, LEADING, IMPLEMENTING, AND EVALUATING AN EFFECTIVE PROFESSIONAL DEVELOPMENT PROGRAM

1. *Know the goals and needs of your audience.* As indicated previously, an understanding of the context is essential. If the reading spe-

cialist is conducting a program in his or her own school, such knowledge is easier to come by than if the program is to be developed for
another school or district. This information might be obtained by inter-
viewing administrators or teachers, visiting the school, or observing in
the classrooms. Lyons and Pinnell (2001) provide an excellent list of
characteristics to look for in the school culture (see Table 5.1).

2. *Hold sessions in environments that are conducive to learning.* In
the LEADERS initiative, we designed the room in which we held sessions to look like the classroom that we expected teachers to have:
There were learning centers, reading and writing areas, and examples of
student work on the wall and boards. The room was equipped with tables so that there was opportunity for group work and discussion. The
environment was a comfortable one that enabled participants to interact
as a community of learners. (Every so often, we had to work in a classroom with individual desks set in rows, and the difference in the interaction and attitude of participants was remarkable!)

It is also important to think about the physical needs of the participants. Plan for breaks and refreshments, as needed. My initial
work with professional development was done with a colleague who
always said, "You have to feed your group!" Although we chuckled
about that statement, it is true that teachers who come to a Saturday
workshop or who need to attend a professional development meeting
after school really need—and enjoy—light refreshments. It not only
meets an actual physical need but also provides an opportunity for social bonding.

3. *Be aware of the of the learning styles and needs of adults.* Teachers,
as adult learners, bring to the learning experience a variety of experiences, skills, and knowledge that influence how new ideas are received
and the degree to which they acquire and implement new skills. They
bring with them their multiple roles and responsibilities not only as
teachers but also as parents, homemakers, etc. They bring the many experiences they have had in life and work as well as their feelings or
emotions associated with past learning experiences. Teachers participate in professional development for monetary incentives on occasion
but more often because they hope to gain concrete and practical ideas
that will enhance the learning outcomes of their students (Guskey,
1986). Indeed, Guskey (1986) reported evidence that positive change in
"learning outcomes of students generally precedes and may be a
prerequisite to significant change in the beliefs and attitudes of most
teachers" (p. 7). Change is gradual for most teachers and requires a

TABLE 5.1. What to Look for in the School Culture

1. As you enter the building, what do you see?

2. Is there a welcoming atmosphere?

3. Is the building as a whole clean and attractive?

4. Is the school office a welcoming place where people are acknowledged and helped?

5. Are the classrooms, cafeteria, office, and library clean and attractive?

6. Do staff members speak respectfully to students and do students talk in respectful tones to one another?

7. What is happening in the yard or playground? Are students playing? Are teachers interacting with students?

8. Are the students and their community a visible part of the school? Is student work displayed and valued in the corridors, office, library, and other gathering places?

9. How available are books? Can students find books to read in places besides the library?

10. Is the principal accessible? Does the principal interact in a friendly way with students, staff members, and visitors?

11. Do people in the school talk with one another? What do they talk about? Do they talk about their work?

12. Are professional development books and materials available?

13. Do teachers have a place where they can meet and work together? Is it attractive and welcoming?

14. When asked about the school, what do people say? Are their comments positive?

15. When asked about the students in the school, what do people say? Are their comments positive?

16. When asked about the parents and the community, what do people say? Are their comments positive?

*Note.* From Lyons and Pinnell (2001, p. 78). Copyright 2001 by Heinemann Publishing. Reprinted by permission.

well-developed, long-term effort. Guskey also discussed several characteristics of effective staff development efforts: (1) The new program or approach should be presented in a clear, explicit, and concrete manner; (2) personal concerns of teachers must be addressed; and (3) the person presenting the program should be credible, articulate, and able to describe how the practice can be used by teachers. Even then, most teachers will not leave the meeting convinced that the new ideas will work for them; at best, they will try them!

Some suggestions for making effective presentations to adults are listed in Table 5.2. These suggestions come from my own experience and from *How to Run Seminars and Workshops* (Jolles, 2001), a book that I have found helpful.

4. *Use a variety of activities and approaches, especially those that require active participation on the part of those attending.* People learn best by "doing," and therefore it is critical that professional development sessions provide opportunities for individuals to think about and discuss various aspects of literacy. Approaches that have been successful include the following:

• *Study groups.* When teachers are involved in an activity that is especially meaningful to them, they become more engaged in the process and are generally more willing to apply what they are learning to their classroom practices. Participation in a study group puts teachers in charge of their own learning, providing them with materials that they can read, reflect about and write on, and discuss with others. Groups may be formal ones established by the school district, or they may function informally, with a group of teachers deciding what they will read, when, and how often they will meet. Often there is a designated leader for each meeting who facilitates the discussion by thinking of questions and activities that may be appropriate for the material to be discussed. For those who want more assistance in developing study groups, the

---

**TABLE 5.2. Making Effective Presentations**

1. Create an atmosphere conducive to adult learning; it should be relaxed, yet businesslike. Seating should be conducive to discussion and interaction. Breaks and refreshments should be planned.

2. Stimulate and maintain interest. Use visuals to reinforce learning; tell stories; ask questions of the group or use small group activities.

3. Involve participants to engender interest and increase retention. In addition to small-group activities and questioning, the learner can ask participants to perform some task.

4. Set your goals and inform participants (i.e., what do you expect them to know or do when the session is over?).

5. Show enthusiasm and use your voice effectively.

6. Plan your session so that you know how much time you will give to each segment.

7. Create a strong beginning and ending. This is where you capture the attention of the group and what the group will remember when they leave!

---

International Reading Association has prepared materials, entitled IRA Literacy Study Groups, that address various aspects of literacy, including vocabulary, beginning reading, and comprehension. The Facilitator's Guide (Irwin, 2002) to these study groups provides a thorough description of how to develop, sustain, and share study group experiences.

• *Analyzing student work.* In LEADERS, teachers brought samples of their students' work and discussed them with others who taught at the same grade level but at different schools. This activity always provided much discussion and reflection, with teachers able to think about how well their students were doing in comparison to those in other classrooms. More importantly, teachers discussed what strategies and activities were helpful in promoting successful performance.

• *Use of videos (classroom practices).* There is no doubt that "seeing is believing." Although we often modeled new strategies for teachers, they always appreciated seeing teachers demonstrate specific strategies with their students. In the beginning, we used tapes that had been developed for other purposes; as we continued with LEADERS, we were able to show tapes that had been made by teachers participating in the project.

• *Use of technology.* Technology can certainly be used in many different ways to enhance the professional development effort. We developed a website for LEADERS (*www.education.pitt.edu/leaders*) and a private listserve that teachers could use to communicate with others. In addition, there were opportunities for teachers to use the Internet to locate resources that would enhance their reading instruction. Several valuable websites include:

> International Reading Association; Read, Write, Think: *http://www.readwritethink.org/*
> Reading Rockets: *http://www.readingrockets.org/*
> America Reads; Resources: *http://www.ed.gov/inits/americareads/resources.html*
> Center for Improvement of Early Reading Achievement: *http://www.ciera.org/*

• *Action research.* When teachers are given opportunities to raise and answer questions they have about their students' learning, they become the ultimate professional. They implement best practices and then assess their effectiveness. In LEADERS, we created a simple framework based on four questions for helping teachers think about their projects:

What do your students need to become better readers or writers?

What activities or strategies are you going to use to help students
succeed?

What was the outcome? What effect did your intervention have on
students?

What have you learned about yourself and your teaching?

Teacher research generates ongoing learning and may facilitate
much change in classroom practice. Teachers interested in such activities need to be encouraged and supported in their efforts. They can discuss their work with other teachers in faculty meetings; they may write
a short column for the school or community newspaper; they can collaborate with others to investigate a specific issue; as in LEADERS, they
may develop posters that display evidence of their work and its effect on
classroom performance. For those interested in reading more about
teacher research, the book by Cochran-Smith and Lytle (1993) is an excellent resource.

• *Reflection.* Give teachers opportunities to discuss and reflect
upon what they have done in their classrooms. They may keep logs or
they can be given opportunities to talk informally with their peers about
their experiences. One of the greatest opportunities for reflection is after teaching a lesson (discussed further in Chapter 6).

5. *Provide opportunities for teachers to receive feedback about implementation in the classroom.* In LEADERS, whenever coaches observed
teachers, they met with them to discuss the results of the observation
(discussed further in Chapter 6).

6. *Provide for evaluation of the professional development initiative.*
Both formative and summative approaches to professional development
are essential. *Formative,* or ongoing, evaluation provides opportunities
for modification, adaptation, or change. *Summative* evaluation, which
addresses impact and results, enables the developer to determine the effect of the professional development effort on individuals and on the
system as a whole. Guskey (2000) identified five levels of evaluation:
participants' reactions, participants' learning, organizational support
and change, participants' use of new knowledge and skills, and student
learning outcomes.

In LEADERS, we used the following techniques for addressing each of the levels:

| | |
|---|---|
| Level 1. Participants' reactions | Questionnaires at end of each workshop |
| | Midyear focus group |
| Level 2. Participants' learning | Teacher Content Test (pre–post) |
| Level 3. Organizational support and change | Interviews/questionnaires with principals and teachers |
| Level 4. Use of new knowledge | Classroom observations |
| Level 5. Student learning | Pre–post tests (LEADERS assessment battery) |

## SUMMARY

In this chapter, I discussed the importance of professional development, describing various models and the standards of the National Staff Development Council that can be used in developing and evaluating such initiatives. LEADERS, a professional development project whose purpose is to improve the literacy teaching of primary teachers, is described to provide a specific illustration of one long-term, intensive effort. Guidelines for developing, leading, implementing, and evaluating an effective professional development program are then presented.

### Reflections

Discuss with your classmates professional development in which you have participated. What activities did you find to be most useful? What, in your view, was least useful?

### Activities

1. Interview an administrator at your school about the professional development plan for teachers in the school, especially as it relates to literacy instruction. Think about whether that plan addresses content, context, and process standards, as developed by the National Staff Development Council.
2. Prepare a professional development session for your classmates (or for

the teachers in your school), in which you introduce them to one new idea or strategy. Use information from the guidelines in this chapter to develop that presentation. Ask the participants to evaluate the session, using a short questionnaire. Then self-evaluate your performance, reflecting on the ideas presented in this chapter.

# 6

## Coaching
### Improving Classroom Literacy Instruction

One criticism of professional development programs is the lack of ongoing support for implementation efforts. Without such support, teachers may have difficulty implementing the strategies or approaches to which they have been introduced and therefore choose to revert to approaches with which they are familiar. For this reason many schools have begun employing literacy coaches when they adopt new approaches; these coaches work with teachers to assist them with their implementation efforts. Furthermore, in current legislation, *Reading First*, there is much support for literacy coaches who can provide professional development in the schools.

The term "literacy coach" is quite appropriate in many ways—especially if we think of the definition of a coach as one with expertise who provides the guidance or feedback that enables someone else to become more proficient. Even as we think of the great football coaches—Vince Lombardi (Green Bay Packers), Chuck Noll (Pittsburgh Steelers), and Ara Parsegian (Notre Dame)—we think of individuals who were not only able to teach in the traditional sense but were able to inspire and motivate their players to do their very best, to live up to their potential.

So it is with literacy coaches: Their job is to work with teachers in their schools and to help them do their very best to facilitate student achievement. These teachers may be novices, needing a great deal of feedback or guidance, or they may be more experienced, having taught for many years. The experienced teachers may need some reinforcement or reassurance, or even some motivation, that will enable them to continue their efforts.

Educators in the field do not always define the word *coach* in a similar fashion. To some, literacy coaches are teachers who coach children, enabling them to do better. Others see them as teachers with expertise in reading (often, reading specialists) who have multiple responsibilities, from working with paraprofessionals or community agencies to working with teachers in the role described above—primarily responsible for providing support and guidance to teachers, so that classroom instruction for students is effective.

The coaching role can vary, depending not only on the job requirements of the coach or reading specialist but on the "readiness" of the teacher. For example, reading specialists can serve as a resource to teachers by providing materials or suggestions for working with struggling readers; they can attend or lead study group meetings, conduct professional development workshops, or just sit and listen to a teacher who wants to discuss ways that he or she can improve instructional practices. (Each of these dimensions is addressed in other chapters.) In this chapter, I focus on two specific aspects of coaching: (1) modeling or demonstrating various instructional approaches and (2) participating in a coaching cycle or conversation that includes observing in the classroom. Such observations can provide teachers with job-embedded professional development that can greatly influence their classroom practices. I begin the chapter with a description of essential characteristics of those who have responsibility for coaching and identify several principles of coaching. This is followed with a discussion of demonstration and observations, as well as by ideas for providing feedback to teachers.

## CHARACTERISTICS OF EFFECTIVE COACHES

The literature on leadership and supervision, as well as my own research in the schools, highlights three important qualifications of literacy coaches.

1. *Know your stuff.* As one principal put it, it is a given that literacy coaches have excellent, up-to-date knowledge of literacy instruction and assessment and the research that undergirds that knowledge. Coaches need this knowledge in order to analyze the lessons they see and identify the relevant aspects of instruction for discussion with the teacher. Those who have a deep understanding of their field are able to "see" things that novices or those with less understanding do not see. An analogy might be a golf instructor who quickly sees that the student is bending his or her arms (not good), not keeping the lower body stable and balanced, or making some other mistake. Likewise, the literacy coach can readily observe, for example, (1) when a teacher moves too quickly through a lesson so that students do not understand and (2) where the teacher might have stopped to check for understanding or (3) provided additional examples of a specific concept or skill. Clearly, reading specialists must be learners themselves, reading the current literature and research and attending conferences and workshops. Certainly, reading specialists must maintain their own professional libraries and join professional organizations, such as the International Reading Association or the National Council of Teachers of English, so that they remain knowledgeable in their field (more about the reading specialist as a lifelong learner in Chapter 11).

2. *Experience.* Literacy coaches are more effective if they have had successful experiences as teachers. Although longevity is not an issue, literacy coaches should have the experience that makes them creditable with classroom teachers and enables them to feel empathy for the teachers' many responsibilities. Some can transcend the need for experience, but in the long run, reading specialists benefit from having worked with classrooms of students with all their diverse needs and interests.

3. *Ability to work with adults.* To function successfully as a coach who has responsibility for observing and giving feedback to teachers, the reading specialist must have excellent interpersonal and communication skills. Coaches must be good listeners, be able to empathize with the teachers, and provide balanced feedback that reinforces excellent teaching behavior and provides ideas for improvement. They must also be able to develop a trusting relationship with the teachers whom they coach, so that their feedback is valued. Essentially, coaches must be able to get their messages across to their colleagues, teachers in the classrooms.

Identified below are some principles that should be taken into consideration when one is involved in coaching activities.

1. *Share your plans and ideas with teachers.* Teachers should understand what such a process means and what it does not mean, why they are involved, and how it will benefit their students. Teachers need to understand that the coaching process is not an evaluative one, but rather one that will enable them to do their job more effectively. To the degree possible, teachers should be invited to participate since they will be more receptive to the process.

2. *Obtain teacher input.* Take time to hear and respond to teachers' concerns. Furthermore, by addressing teachers' needs, coaching will be much more effective.

3. *Provide necessary support.* Once the coaching process begins, it is important to provide the resources that teachers need if they are going to make changes in their classroom instruction. In other words, if a coach identifies a specific need (e.g., additional training or supplemental material), such support should be provided.

4. *Take time to develop the trust needed to be an effective coach.* Begin with those who are eager and willing to participate. By working with teachers who are receptive, coaches themselves will be more relaxed and can use these initial cycles as opportunities to practice their "coaching" and communication skills. Furthermore, one will build trust by maintaining confidentiality. Coaches who talk about what they have seen in classrooms will not be seen as individuals whose responsibility is one of providing support. Teachers will be less likely to respond in a positive manner to them.

Some resources that may be helpful to those involved in such coaching are *Cognitive Coaching* (Costa & Garmston, 2002) and *How to Implement a Peer Coaching Program* (Robbins, 1991).

In the following sections, I focus on two essential tasks specifically related to job-embedded coaching: demonstrations and observations.

## DEMONSTRATING OR MODELING

One of the most important means of coaching is demonstrating or modeling specific behaviors or strategies. As mentioned previously, Fullan (1991) described the "implementation dip" that often occurs in our schools. Specifically, he discusses the fact that even after teachers have attended workshops or presentations about effective programs or approaches, their successful implementation of what they learned remains an issue. So, if the goal is to have a teacher learn to use a specific strategy, such as Ogle's (1986) K-W-L, the coach may need to model that approach while the teacher observes. In the LEADERS project, described in Chapter 5, participating teachers indicated that demonstration lessons were extremely helpful for them. When they saw another individual using a specific approach or strategy, especially in their own classrooms, these teachers felt as though they had a much better understanding of how to implement that strategy. Some guidelines for giving such demonstration lessons follow:

1. Plan with teachers so that they have some role in the lesson, assisting children or conducting a small part of the lesson. This active involvement creates much more interest and understanding on the part of the teacher—as well as commitment.

2. Discuss the lesson with the teacher as soon as possible after teaching it. Reflect with the teacher on the effectiveness of the lesson. What went well? What could have gone better? Be honest in sharing with the teacher unexpected aspects of the lesson (e.g., handling of a behavior problem, etc.) Not every lesson is perfect (few are, indeed), and teachers will feel much more comfortable working with a coach when they see that the coach also can have difficulty with a disruptive student or elicit little response from students, despite earnest efforts to stimulate interaction. Be sure to give teachers the opportunity to ask questions, reflect, and make comments as well.

3. Arrange for a time to observe the teacher presenting the same type of lesson demonstrated. This is a critical step that helps to ensure that the teacher has actually learned from the demonstration lesson and can implement a strategy correctly.

## OBSERVATIONS

One of the most effective coaching approaches to professional development is observing the work of teachers. It is there that the coach can actually intercede, provide the reinforcement, alter various behaviors, or augment the teaching approaches of those observed. Observations, however, are too often synonymous with evaluation, since frequently that has been their primary purpose. In the coaching model described below, the focus is on facilitating the teacher's growth and the coach is seen as a resource. Indeed, using this coaching model in an evaluative manner distorts its value and hinders the coach from developing the trust and openness necessary for success. Table 6.1 outlines a model for coaching similar to the models proposed by Costa and Garmston (1994) and Glickman (1990). The four steps include planning, observing, analyzing/reflecting, and conferring.

In the following sections, each of the four steps is described, with examples from several coaching "cycles."

## Planning

Planning is an important first step. Walking into the classroom without a focus is similar to traveling in an unfamiliar city without a map and trying to get from one location to another—there are many different directions to take and many different means of transportation. Likewise, with observation. The planning conference enables the coach and the teacher to discuss important issues:

> What are the goals of the lesson?
> What does the teacher hope to gain from the observation?

---

**TABLE 6.1. Coaching Cycle**

Step 1. Planning

Talk with the teacher, using the following questions: What are the goals for the lesson? What does the teacher hope to gain from the experience? In what ways should data be collected?

Step 2. Observing

Observe in the classroom, focusing on the aspects that have been jointly agreed upon in the planning meeting.

Step 3. Analyzing/reflecting

Both coach and teacher think about the lesson that has been observed. The coach analyzes data from observation and identifies topics/issues for discussion. The teacher generates questions and ideas for discussion.

Step 4. Conferring

Coach and teacher meet to discuss the lesson, using data obtained in steps 2 and 3. The goal of this step is to obtain a commitment from the teacher as to what aspects will be applied in future lessons.

---

What is the best means of obtaining the information needed to address the teacher's goals?

What are the procedures to be followed? (e.g., Where should the coach sit? How long should the coach stay?)

The planning session provides an opportunity for building trust and promoting reflection. It also enables the coach to learn things about the class, the lesson, and the teacher that could be helpful. For example, this may be the first lesson that the teacher has taught using a particular strategy; or perhaps there is a student with special needs who just arrived 2 days ago. One planning meeting between a second-grade teacher and a coach went as follows:

> Sally, a second-grade teacher, was trying an approach new to her: teaching a mini-lesson on writing, specifically report writing. She was not certain how to present the material effectively and wanted Teresa, the coach, to provide her with some feedback. Sally and Teresa agreed that Teresa would observe, noting the procedures that Sally used in teaching the lesson. They agreed that Teresa needed to attend to the behavior of the students to determine whether they understood and were involved in the lesson. Teresa indicated that she would "script" the lesson, trying to record exactly what Sally and the students were doing at significant points in the lesson. Sally reminded Teresa that she would be working with the entire class and that her class was not familiar with how to write reports. This would be an introductory lesson. They agreed on a time and place for the observation.

## Carrying out the Observation

Many excellent texts provide a great deal of information on approaches to observation: Glickman (1990), Costa and Garmston (1994), and Lyons and Pinnell (2001), to cite a few. There are also many different data collection tools, including audio and video recordings, frequency counts of various behaviors, checklists, and complete scripting of teacher verbal behaviors. Some of these techniques are very comprehensive and time consuming; others, less so. In this text I describe one approach that can be useful for the observations that literacy coaches typically make, given their major foci on instructional strategies, effective classroom management, and classroom environments that best enhance students' literacy achievement. I also identify several other observation systems that have been developed specifically for literacy instruction; however, these are somewhat complex and probably more useful when a more comprehensive analysis of classroom instruction is needed. Described below are three important aspects of classroom instruction that can be observed.

## Classroom Environment

There is clear evidence that effective teachers design their classrooms in ways to promote literacy. For example, many children's books are available and easily accessible—not hidden away where students cannot get to them. Student work is prominently displayed; in fact, there is more student work than commercial posters and charts. The presence of small-group work or learning centers indicates teachers' respect and appreciation for productive social interaction among small groups of students focused on an educational endeavor. Posted literacy standards further help students understand what is expected of them.

## Classroom Management

Taylor, Pressley, and Pearson (2002) indicated that the management systems of effective teachers are so subtle that one is not aware that such a system exists. In other words, students know the routines and the teacher's behavioral expectations. They move from task to task without chaos or confusion There is a positive tone in the classroom, as the teacher provides reinforcement and reassurance to guide the work of students. Students are respectful of the teacher and each other. In one first-grade classroom in which I observed, the teacher never raised her voice; she was conferring with individual students while pairs of students worked together at the chalkboard. As I marveled at this well orchestrated community of learners, she commented, "Too often, these children are subjected to yelling and screaming at home; they seem to appreciate the quiet of this classroom."

## Instruction

Since their role is to assist teachers in mastering new or different strategies being promoted in the school, one of the major areas that literacy coaches must address is that of instruction. It is here that the coaches can use their knowledge and understanding of reading instruction to determine whether the teachers are implementing strategies in an efficient and effective manner. In addition, literacy coaches also can assist teachers by attending to two other aspects of teaching: (1) responding to students' errors, and (2) maintaining active involvement.

*Responding to Student Error.* As teachers, we often solicit responses from students to determine their understanding as well as to maintain attention. What happens when a student responds with an incorrect answer? Does the teacher quickly call on another student, or is there "scaffolding" in place that enables the student to answer correctly? Is scaffolding done quickly and effectively so that the attention of the class is maintained? Recently, I watched a first-grade teacher as she listened to students reading a selection. She quickly and efficiently helped students when they made errors in oral reading. In some cases, she told the student the word; in other cases, she asked them to try to sound it out (e.g., "Take off the ending . . . think of that word family at the end"); and in other situations, she mentioned that the student should think about what makes sense. All of this was done so effectively that all those in the group remained attentive to the story being read.

*Maintaining Active Involvement of Students.* Although teachers may implement a strategy or approach in an appropriate manner, difficulties with student attention still may arise. This difficulty is especially likely to occur when teachers are working with the entire class, and the lesson does not address the individual needs of students. It is critical that the coach work with the teacher so that active involvement can be maintained. When the inattention of students becomes obvious, teachers need to be encouraged to think of ways to stimulate mental and physical alertness. Adjusting lesson content, small-group or partner work, the use of manipulatives, and physical participation can be discussed in the postobservation conference.

## Conducting Observations

As mentioned previously, there are many different frameworks or systems that can be used for collecting data during observations. The one described below requires the coach to describe what is happening—not to interpret or make judgments *about* what is happening. Using paper and pen or with a laptop computer, the coach records exactly what is going on in the classroom. The end product provides the coach with "data" that can be shared with the classroom teacher; for example, "Here's what the students were doing when. . . . " Specific steps are summarized in Table 6.2.

When entering the classroom, it is best to remain as unobtrusive as possible, finding a spot to sit and observe without interrupting the flow of the lesson. There are times, however, when the teacher will choose to introduce the coach/specialist; if so, smiling, greeting the students, and then finding a place to sit and watch is recommended. There are also occasions when the teacher attempts to have the coach interact with the students and the lesson. In those instances, the coach may choose to join in and actually help teach the lesson. The teacher can learn a great deal by having the coach work with him or her, and since the coach's goal is to be helpful to the teacher, this modification may be just what is needed at this time. Depending upon the coach's job responsibilities, he or she may also have to return to observe the teacher doing the lesson unaided! In that case, the teacher should be told that in the next lesson, the coach/reading specialist will need to observe and not participate.

It does take time to learn to observe using this approach. However, with practice it becomes a very effective means of collecting the information needed to interact effectively with teachers.

## Other Observation Systems

The observation form in Figure 6.1 was used in the collection of data for an evaluation project in which we observed classroom literacy instruction in grades K–8 (Bean, Eichelberger, Turner, & Tellez, 2002). This form was influenced by the work of Taylor and Pearson (2002); several of the categories and specific behaviors from their School Change Classroom Observation Scheme have been adapted for use. The form can also be useful for thinking about the various dimensions to be observed (e.g., instruction, materials, classroom management, etc.). Reading specialists may also be interested in the framework developed by Henk, Moore, Marinak, and Tomasetti (2000), described in Figure 6.2. This is a useful framework for discussing best practices with teachers. It can be a great resource for a professional development session, in which teachers talk about what each of the statements mean and the importance of those activities to effective literacy instruction.

**TABLE 6.2. Observation System for Data Collection**

1. Upon entering the room, spend several minutes doing an environmental sweep and collecting information about number of students, literacy environment in the room, and seating arrangements. You may want to draw a picture of the classroom.

2. Using blank sheets of paper, divide the sheet into two sections with a line down the middle, with a T for teacher in the left section and an S for students in the right section.

3. Begin identifying what is occurring in the classroom. If there is classroom discourse (i.e., the teacher is interacting with the students), try to jot down key phrases or words that the teacher and the students are saying. You may also want to identify whether specific students are responding. Remember to note whatever is especially relevant to the focus or goal identified in the planning session. For example, if the teacher wants the coach to attend to levels of questions, then recording the specific questions is important. If the teacher wants the coach to observe whether students are actively involved, then the coach would need to attend to that dimension of instruction. At the same time, observing what is happening overall may be the key to identifying why students are not actively involved.

4. When the teacher is serving more as a facilitator, the coach can focus on what students are doing, or not doing, as well as what the teacher is doing.

Example of a script:

| Teacher | Students |
| --- | --- |
| *Walking around helping students, answering questions.* | *Students are all writing in their journals.* |
| *Helps child by asking him to read what he had written in journal.* | *One student has head down and is not writing. (OC: task too difficult?)* |

5. Every 5 minutes, draw a line under what you have written so that you have some indication of how long various activities have lasted and when they occurred. Sometimes, you may want to draw a line when an activity changes; for example, the teacher has finished reading a story and is now beginning to ask questions about the selection.

6. Mark "OC" (observer's comment) when there are events in the lesson about which you want to talk with the teacher or have questions. For example, mark "OC" next to the note, "Student refused to do work" and note query, "Can't do?"

7. Every 5 minutes or so (when it seems appropriate), it is wise to stop writing and just look around the classroom. It is easy to become so immersed in the writing that you miss some of the nonverbal and physical interactions.

Name:_____Grade:___School:_____Subject:_____

## Instruction
Evidence of:
_____student engagement
_____clarity of explanations/directions
        (helping students understand)
_____ modeling/coaching/scaffolding
_____flexible grouping

Specific strategies observed:


Comments:


## Grouping
___whole class
___small group
___pairs
___individual
___other

## Materials
___text
___student writing
___board/chart
___worksheet
___games
___other

## Classroom Management
Evidence that the teacher:
_____uses positive reinforcement
_____exhibits positive-feeling tone
_____establishes clear expectations for behavior
_____establishes routines that students understand

Comments:


## Teacher Interaction
___tell/give information
___modeling
___recitation
___discussion
___coaching/scaffolding
___listening/watching
___reading aloud
___check work (monitoring)
___other

## Literate Environment
Evidence of:
_____student work around the room
_____classroom libraries
_____places for small-group work (reading center,
        learning centers, etc.)
_____print-rich
_____standards/expectations for students

## Student Response
___reading
___reading turn-taking
___talking
___listening
___writing
___manipulating

Code: 0 = not at all evident; 1 = evident sometimes;
        2 = evident most of the time; 3 = evident throughout

Comments:

| Time period | 1 | 2 | 3 | 4 | 5 | 6 |
|---|---|---|---|---|---|---|
| Students on task | | | | | | |
| 75% or more students on task | | | | | | |
| 50–75% students on task | | | | | | |
| Less than 50% students on task | | | | | | |

FIGURE 6.1. Classroom Observation Form.

Teacher_____Observer_____
School year _____ Date of observation _____ Observation # _____
Observation occurred: Before reading _____ During reading _____ After reading _____

## Component I. Classroom Climate

O  C  R  N

A. Many different types of authentic reading materials such as magazines, newspapers, novels, and nonfiction works are displayed and are available for children to read independently.  ☐ ☐ ☐ ☐

B. The classroom has a reading area such as a corner or classroom library where children are encouraged to go to read for enjoyment.  ☐ ☐ ☐ ☐

C. An area is available for small-group reading instruction.  ☐ ☐ ☐ ☐

D. Active participation and social interaction are integral parts of reading instruction in this classroom.  ☐ ☐ ☐ ☐

E. The classroom environment indicates that reading and writing are valued and actively promoted (e.g., purposeful writing is displayed, journals are maintained, Word Walls are used, book talks and read-alouds by teacher occur regularly).  ☐ ☐ ☐ ☐

## Component II. Prereading Phase

O  C  R  N

A. During the prereading discussion, the teacher asked the children to preview the text by having them read the title of the selection, look at the illustrations, and then discuss the possible contents of the text.  ☐ ☐ ☐ ☐

B. Children were encouraged to activate their background knowledge through the use of K-W-L charts, webs, anticipation guides, etc.  ☐ ☐ ☐ ☐

C. By generating a discussion about the topic before reading the selection, the teacher created an interest in the reading.  ☐ ☐ ☐ ☐

D. The teacher introduced and discussed the new vocabulary words in a meaningful context, focusing on those new words that were central to the understanding of the story.  ☐ ☐ ☐ ☐

E. The children were encouraged to state or write predictions related to the topic of the reading selection.  ☐ ☐ ☐ ☐

F. Before reading occurred, the teacher helped the children identify the type of material that was to be read to determine what their purpose should be for reading it.  ☐ ☐ ☐ ☐

G. The objective for the reading lesson was clearly identified for the children, along with how the objective related to previous lessons.  ☐ ☐ ☐ ☐

H. The teacher continually assessed children's prereading discussion and made appropriate adjustments.  ☐ ☐ ☐ ☐

**FIGURE 6.2.** The Reading Lesson Observation Format. From Henk, Moore, Marinak, and Tomasetti (2000, pp. 360–362). Copyright 2000 by the International Reading Association. Reprinted by permission.

(continued)

**Component III. Guided Reading Phase**     O   C   R   N

A. At appropriate points during the reading of the selection, the   ☐   ☐   ☐   ☐
children were asked to evaluate their initial predictions.

B. The children were asked to identify or read aloud portions of   ☐   ☐   ☐   ☐
text that confirmed or disproved predictions they had made
about the selection.

C. The comprehension discussion focused on the purposes that   ☐   ☐   ☐   ☐
were established for reading the selection.

D. An appropriate mix of factual and higher-level thinking   ☐   ☐   ☐   ☐
questions were incorporated into the comprehension
discussion.

E. During the reading lesson, the teacher modeled fluent reading   ☐   ☐   ☐   ☐
and then encouraged the children to read fluently and with
expression.

F. The teacher encouraged the children to adjust their reading   ☐   ☐   ☐   ☐
rate to fit the material.

G. The teacher monitored the children and gave proper assistance   ☐   ☐   ☐   ☐
and feedback while they read or completed practice activities.

H. The teacher modeled and encouraged the use of new   ☐   ☐   ☐   ☐
vocabulary during the discussion.

I. The children were encouraged to use a variety of word study   ☐   ☐   ☐   ☐
strategies (e.g., words within words, context, syllabication) to
decipher the meaning of unknown words as appropriate.

J. The children were encouraged to use appropriate   ☐   ☐   ☐   ☐
comprehension monitoring and fix-up strategies during reading
(e.g., paraphrasing, rereading, using context, asking for help).

K. The teacher reminded the children to make use of their   ☐   ☐   ☐   ☐
knowledge of text structure (e.g., fictional story grammar,
nonfiction text structures).

L. The teacher periodically assessed the children's ability to   ☐   ☐   ☐   ☐
monitor meaning.

**Component IV. Postreading Phase**     O   C   R   N

A. During the postreading discussion, the children were asked to   ☐   ☐   ☐   ☐
read aloud sections of the text that substantiated answers to
questions and confirmed or disproved predictions they had
made about the selection.

B. The teacher asked the children to retell the material they had   ☐   ☐   ☐   ☐
read, concentrating on major events or concepts.

C. The children were asked to explain their opinion and critical   ☐   ☐   ☐   ☐
judgments.

D. The teacher had the children provide a written response to the   ☐   ☐   ☐   ☐
reading (e.g., written retelling, written summarization, written
evaluation).

*(continued)*

E. Children were encouraged to use new vocabulary in written responses. Examples and modeling were provided by the teacher. ☐ ☐ ☐ ☐

F. Writing was used as a natural extension of reading tasks. ☐ ☐ ☐ ☐

G. The teacher continually monitored children's comprehension and provided appropriate feedback. ☐ ☐ ☐ ☐

### Component V. Skill and Strategy Instruction

        O  C  R  N

A. The teacher provided a clear explanation about the structure of the skill or strategy to be learned and described when and how it could be used. ☐ ☐ ☐ ☐

B. The teacher modeled the use of the skill or strategy so children were able to see how it would be used in an appropriate situation. ☐ ☐ ☐ ☐

C. Any direct teaching of a phonemic element was immediately followed by children using the skill in a meaningful context. ☐ ☐ ☐ ☐

D. Explicit skill and strategy instruction was provided and applied in the context of the reading selection. ☐ ☐ ☐ ☐

E. The children were encouraged to use before, during, and after reading strategies as appropriate. ☐ ☐ ☐ ☐

F. Reading skill and strategy instruction moved children toward independent use through scaffolding. ☐ ☐ ☐ ☐

### Component VI. Materials and Tasks of the Lesson

        O  C  R  N

A. The selections used for the reading lesson were appropriate for children of this ability and grade level. ☐ ☐ ☐ ☐

B. The reading materials represented authentic types of texts. ☐ ☐ ☐ ☐

C. Reading materials and tasks reflected a sensitivity to the diverse learning needs of the children. ☐ ☐ ☐ ☐

D. The amount and type of independent work was appropriate for the level of the children and instructional goals it was designed to achieve. ☐ ☐ ☐ ☐

E. Independent work often contained open-ended questions that encouraged children to enhance and extend their understanding of the selection. ☐ ☐ ☐ ☐

F. The literacy tasks the children were asked to perform during the lesson were meaningful and relevant. ☐ ☐ ☐ ☐

G. The children engaged in various modes of reading during the lesson (e.g., silent, oral, guided, shared). ☐ ☐ ☐ ☐

H. The teacher provided opportunities for the children to read for enjoyment. ☐ ☐ ☐ ☐

I. Children were encouraged to respond personally or creatively to the reading material. ☐ ☐ ☐ ☐

J. A balance existed in the reading lesson between teacher-initiated and student-initiated activities. ☐ ☐ ☐ ☐

K. Reading materials and tasks were organized around themes  □ □ □ □
   when appropriate.

**Component VII. Teacher Practices**                         O  C  R  N

A. The teacher focused on reading as a meaningful process.   □ □ □ □

B. The instructional techniques used by the teacher and the ways  □ □ □ □
   they were executed reflected an awareness of recommended
   practices.

C. Children were grouped appropriately and flexibly.         □ □ □ □

D. The teacher's management of the reading lesson provided for  □ □ □ □
   active student engagement.

E. The pace and flow of the various phases of the reading lesson  □ □ □ □
   represented an effective use of time.

F. The teacher's instruction was sensitive to the diversity of  □ □ □ □
   children's experiences and their social, cultural, ethnic, and
   linguistic needs.

G. The teacher actively promoted the integration of the language  □ □ □ □
   arts in this lesson.

H. The teacher encouraged the children to take informed risks  □ □ □ □
   and promoted safe failure.

I. The teacher's conferences with children were timely, focused,  □ □ □ □
   and positive in nature.

J. Authentic assessment practices were used in this lesson.   □ □ □ □

K. The teacher's planned goals, actual instruction, and       □ □ □ □
   assessment practices were aligned.

**Key to checklist**

O = Observed        This component was observed and was judged to be of
                    satisfactory quality.
C = Commendation    This component was observed and was judged to be of very
                    *high* quality.
R = Recommendation  This component either was not observed or was judged to be
                    of unsatisfactory quality.
N = Not applicable  This component was not observed because it was not
                    appropriate for the lesson.

## Analyzing/Reflecting

Each step of the coaching cycle is an important one; however, the step
of analyzing/reflecting is critical, for without it, there is little chance of
facilitating an impact on teacher performance. Reflection is not only the
purview of the coach but also of the teacher. Before meeting for a
postconference, both literacy coach and teacher must think about what
occurred in the lesson, and especially in what ways the questions raised
in the preconference or planning stage can be addressed. The literacy

coach may ask the teacher to jot down a few ideas, or such a question may be raised in the conference itself. The coach should take time before the conference to analyze what has been observed.

It is here, in the analysis phase, that the coach can make good use of the notes or scripts that were written during the observation. These notes provide excellent information that can be shared with the teacher during the conference. What levels of questions did the teacher ask? What steps did he or she follow in teaching the strategy? How many students (and who) were not involved during the lesson? Going back through the notes and thinking about answers to the following questions enable the coach to plan a strategy for the postconference to be held with the teacher:

> What are the key points to raise? (What factors are most important in terms of possible impact on student learning?)
>
> How do I want to start the conference? (Do I start with identification of some strengths? Can I ask the teacher to discuss his or her views?)
>
> What changes would best improve the instruction going on in that classroom? Are the changes doable? What support would be needed by the teacher to implement the changes?
>
> What approach might be best in working with this teacher?

## Conferring

The postconference should occur as close in time to the actual observation as possible, not only to allay the teacher's concerns, but also because recall and memory of what occurred is so much better. However, the analysis and reflection step is important and should not be eliminated. I find it helpful to talk briefly with teachers immediately after an observation, thanking them for the opportunity to work with them and making a positive comment about some aspect of the lesson (the classroom environment, one student's performance, etc.)

One goal of the conference is to promote teacher reflection to the highest degree possible, focusing on teacher and student behaviors (who was doing what?); comparing actual and desired behaviors; considering reasons why these occurred or did not occur.

One of the most important goals of the postconference is the generation of future plans: What can the teacher take back from the conference that will facilitate instruction in the classroom? Another goal is to assess the effects of the coaching experience: In what ways was the experience helpful—and what comes next?

Coaches need to be cognizant of the individual strengths, experiences, and learning styles of teachers. Using this knowledge, coaches can work with teachers in one of three ways: as a mirror, as a collaborator, and as an expert (Robbins, 1991).

## Coach as Mirror

In this instance, the teacher is self-reflective and quickly assumes a leadership role in the conference. The coach then serves to confirm and validate what the teacher articulates. These types of conferences generally move along quite easily, because the teacher sees his or her own strengths and weaknesses and actually raises possible solutions to any difficulties that occur. The coach then serves as a mirror by reflecting back to the teacher specific examples that indicate support for what the teacher is saying. In the example below, the coach is working with an experienced kindergarten teacher who analyzes her own behavior and sets future goals for herself.

KINDERGARTEN TEACHER: I lost the group after about 15 minutes. They were really with me until I started asking various questions about the main character. I don't think they lost interest in the story. I think they were sitting too long. I wonder if I might have asked several of them to . . .

COACH: Yes, I think you're right. After about the third question, when you were trying . . .

## Coach as Collaborator

In this case, the literacy coach and teacher work together to determine the strengths and possible weaknesses of the lessons. They are both struggling to identify what was especially effective and what may have been done better.

THIRD-GRADE TEACHER: It seems to me that there has to be a better way to get more students involved in the discussion. It seems as though the same students are always raising their hands, while the others wait for them to reply.

COACH: Let's talk about this. Remember reading that article about holding effective discussions in the classroom? Let's think about those recommendations. One suggestion was that the teacher ask students to talk to each other before . . .

TEACHER: Oh, yes! That's a great idea. Another thought was to ask students to generate questions for other students. Goodness, let's talk about how I might do that.

*Coach as Expert*

In some instances, especially with novice teachers or teachers who are attempting a new approach for the first time, the coach may need to serve as expert: as the individual who can provide information that helps teachers understand whether they are implementing various strategies or approaches effectively.

FIFTH-GRADE TEACHER: So, when I was trying the K-W-L, I wasn't sure what I should do after students identified all they knew about turtles. Exactly how should I move to the W step?

COACH: I think you did a great job! You had the students review what they knew, and then you commented: "Wow, we know a lot, but it appears that there is still much more to learn. For example, I wondered what the differences were between land turtles and sea turtles? What are some things you are wondering about?" You helped to jump-start the students!

## GIVING FEEDBACK

The feedback that coaches provide to teachers about their instructional practices may require teachers to consider some changes in what or how they teach. If the teacher and coach together can identify those areas or behaviors in which change is desired (i.e., coach as mirror or coach as collaborator), then the feedback session is generally a productive and positive one. On the other hand, there are times when the coach has to be more direct in working with a teacher. Always, the desire is to provide feedback that is constructive and workable. Nevertheless, some teachers may react defensively and be unable to accept or benefit from feedback, unless it is provided in a carefully balanced manner. Several suggestions for giving feedback follow.

1. *Be specific.* Telling the teacher that the lesson was good, fine, or interesting is not constructive—it does not provide information the teacher can use to improve classroom practices. Instead the coach might describe what made the classroom an attractive place for learning (e.g., many different kinds of books in places where students could readily access them; student work posted on the walls; a chart that read "You Made My Day," with students' names on it).

2. *Behave in ways that reduce defensive behavior.* It is natural for all of us to defend what we have done in response to what we perceive as a criticism. Coaches can reduce defensive behavior in several ways. First, they can focus on describing what they observed rather than making a judgment about it and, to the degree possible, create a problem-solving situation (e.g., "I noticed that students were less attentive in the discussion part of the lesson than when they were reading the story. Let's talk about that. What do you think caused their inattention?"). Such an approach promotes collaboration and reduces the tendency for the coach to be perceived as the only one who has the answers. Second, coaches can acknowledge the fact that the teacher has unique experiences and knowledge that will contribute to the solution of the problem. Teachers know the goals they are trying to achieve and the personalities of the students with whom they work. They can therefore contribute to the solutions or suggestions in ways the coach cannot.

3. *Provide balanced feedback.* Make certain that the teacher clearly understands the issue or item under discussion and how to resolve it. For example, if the teacher is providing opportunities for students to develop fluency, but the students are reading books that are too difficult for them to read without making many errors, the coach needs to make certain that the teacher understands that fluency practice is important and valued but that, in order for it to be productive, the material needs to be at an instructional or independent level. Feedback can be divided into a two-step process, as follows:

a. Discuss the merits of what the teacher is doing (e.g., the merits of providing fluency practice for students).

"We know that in order to be effective readers, students need to have opportunities to practice reading. The use of partner reading is certainly an effective strategy, and so is repeated reading. It was great to see that happening in your classroom."

b. Identify the concern or area that needs changing.

"One of the ways that you can increase the effectiveness of the fluency practice you are providing is by changing the difficulty level of the material that students are using. What materials do you have available that might be appropriate? Or, let's see what is available in the resource room."

Notice that, in the example above, the coach was not critical of the teacher but related information on how the teacher could increase the effect of an important strategy that he or she had attempted in the classroom. Balanced feedback should include specific information as to what is effective and what can be improved. The teacher and coach both should explore ideas for how to address the concern.

Coaching can be a valuable approach to improving the literacy instruction in a school. It can also be a growth experience for both the coach and the teacher. However, given that schools have not generally focused on these types of supportive observations, it takes time to build an atmosphere of trust and receptivity to this approach. In talking with an individual responsible for working with new teachers, I asked her what she thought were the most important components of effective coaching. She shared these comments:

1. *Confidentiality.* What is seen by the coach and said by the teacher always stays between them. Nothing should ever be repeated, criticized, or made fun of in the teachers' lounge, principal's office, or at a school function.

2. *Nonthreatening demeanor.* The coach is present as a colleague, not an evaluator. Bring to the conscious level all of the good things that are happening in the class and offer suggestions about other possible methods of presenting the information. The coach is not there to make a teacher feel incompetent!

3. *Focus.* It is always advantageous to have a mutually agreed-upon target to focus the observation. When the conference occurs, the coach is ready with multiple suggestions and questions designed to make the teacher think and grow professionally (personal communication, 2001).

## SUMMARY

This chapter discussed the importance of coaching as an approach to providing professional development for teachers. In addition to describing the qualifications of effective coaches, the use of demonstration lessons as a means of modeling for teachers was explored. Observing in the classroom as a means of improving classroom teaching practices is emphasized. Steps comprising a coaching cycle involving observations were identified, as was a system for data collection. Lastly, techniques for providing feedback to teachers were presented.

### Reflections

1. Given your experiences, how comfortable would you be observing in a classroom and providing feedback to teachers? What skills do you think you need to develop more fully?
2. Think about the coaching cycle. What would be the most difficult steps for you to implement? Why?

### Activities

1. Go through a coaching cycle with a colleague. Think about the following after you have completed the cycle. What did you learn from the planning conference that affected the way in which you observed? In your analysis of the observation, what points did you identify as important to discuss with the colleague? In what ways did you provide feedback to the teacher? How successful do you think you were in conducting this coaching cycle? What would you do differently?
2. Try providing balanced feedback. Work with a colleague or a member of your class. Here are two scenarios to try. Remember, (1) clarify what has occurred, (2) provide specific feedback about the merits of a situation or behavior, and (3) discuss ways to address any concern.

> *Scenario 1.* Carlos observed Frank, a sixth-grade social studies teacher, as he used an anticipation guide to introduce a new unit on the Civil War. He gave the class a sheet on which there were a number of facts about the war and asked them to indicate whether they agreed or disagreed with the facts. Immediately, hands were raised; students grumbled that they could not read certain words or that they did not know what to do. Frank told them to put the sheet in their desks and to open their books to the first page of the chapter.

*Scenario 2.* Henrietta arrived to observe Greta, a third-grade teacher, who had indicated that she was trying to use flexible grouping in her classroom, but that students were not able to work independently. She wanted help from Henrietta because, at this point, as she stated, "These kids can't work independently." Now Greta was conducting guided reading with a group of six students. On the board was a list indicating what other students should be doing: reading books silently, working on the computer, or doing worksheets. And some were actually doing those things. However, four or five students were wandering around, talking to others. Two had their heads on the desk and appeared to be sleeping. Every 2 minutes or so, Greta would look around, away from the group with whom she was working, and remind students firmly, "You know what you should be doing. Let's get to it!"

# 7

# Developing a School
# Reading Program

The more things change, the more they remain the same.
—ALPHONSE KARR (1849)

The goal of this chapter is to provide information and cultivate awareness about the role of reading specialists in developing and
sustaining an effective reading program in the entire school or district.
In previous chapters, the importance of working with individuals or
small groups as a means of promoting change at the classroom level was
discussed. Although such efforts are important, even for large-scale program improvement, it is also essential that reading specialists be informed about their potential roles in facilitating/promoting total school
or district change. The chapter begins with those issues or problems
that often prevent the development of effective reading programs in
schools. In the following sections, guidelines for effective change are
offered, beginning with a discussion of curriculum and curriculum
development; then suggestions for material selection and usage are presented. A concluding section addresses the importance of familiarity
with the various requirements of state and federal educational agencies.

Schools must adhere to requirements imposed by legislation and address the accountability demanded by these agencies. Often, it is a reading specialist who is responsible for leading the efforts to write district standards, develop the plan for Title 1 programs, or write a proposal to receive additional funding to meet the needs of struggling readers.

## PROBLEMS OF EFFECTING LARGE-SCALE CHANGE

In order to enhance the possibility of success, educators involved in efforts to develop schoolwide reading programs need to be aware of the barriers or issues that create difficulties in school improvement or reform efforts. Fullan (1991), Fullan and Hargreaves (1996), Hall and Hord (1987), and others have written about barriers to educational change. Fullan and Hargreaves identified six basic problems, each of which can be related to school reading program development: overload, isolation, "groupthink," untapped competence (and neglected incompetence), narrowness in teachers' roles, and poor solutions or failed reform (p. 2). Each of these, as they relate to literacy instruction, is discussed below.

### Overload

Teachers are required to do much in today's schools. Not only are they responsible for teaching various subjects or skills, they are also asked to handle students with special needs or serious discipline problems. Some work in schools where there are large numbers of students from poverty backgrounds, which are generally associated with other problems such as lack of positive literacy experiences and poor attendance. Teachers may be asked to learn about and implement many initiatives or programs, some of which are not compatible with each other. Sometimes these initiatives are driven by the funding that is available to school districts, with requirements in the funding regulations. For example, in one district, a school had obtained funding to implement a program based on a form of individually prescribed instruction. At the same time, the district was attempting to implement a form of classroom management that recommended whole-class instruction, with provision for individual differences through multilevel tasks. Teachers were confused and legitimately frustrated in the face of administrative refusal to deal with their concerns, which contended that there was no problem in a marriage of the two initiatives. If this was not enough to cause problems, one of the schools embarked on a writing initiative that required teachers to attend professional development sessions *in addition* to the ones they were attending for the first two initiatives!

## Isolation

A sentiment I hear expressed frequently is: "It doesn't matter what I hear in school meetings; I just shut my door and do what I believe is best." Often, these statements are made with every good intention by teachers who have seen initiatives come—and go! Schools tend to be organized around an isolationist perspective, with each teacher assuming major responsibility for the 25 or more students in his or her classroom. Given the move to inclusion and the increase of in-class programs in literacy instruction, such isolationism is no longer possible. However, it is difficult for some teachers to deal with the fact that they may no longer have sole responsibility for the students in their classroom. Moreover, often these teachers do not have the experiences and training that enable them to participate easily in such programs.

## Groupthink

In today's schools, a great deal of emphasis is placed on developing communities or networks of learners, for example, stressing the importance of collegiality and collaboration in promoting school change. Although such efforts can be powerful forces for change, there are some downsides to them. Fullan and Hargreaves (1996) indicated how important it is to support individual creativity and diversity while, at the same time, enhancing the ability of individuals to work together for change. Once a group establishes a norm, it is often difficult for the creative thinker to be heard. Yet it is this individual who can often bring new and fresh insights to a specific issue.

## Untapped Competence (and Neglected Incompetence)

Each and every educator in the school has the potential to contribute to an effective school reading program and assume a leadership role in creating school change. When school administrations function in ways that limit the extent to which all teachers can participate in the change process, they are choosing to ignore the competence and knowledge of their teachers. Interacting with teachers provides information about activities that work or do not work, instructional strategies that have been modified so that they are more effective for younger or older students, and management techniques that create an atmosphere in which learning can take place. We need to capture the talent that exists in schools, not only to develop effective reading programs, but also to give teachers the sense of pride and ownership that enhances individual classroom instruction. At the same time, we must be bold enough to challenge those few who are incompetent or who refuse to work with students in ways that promote learning.

## Narrowness in Teachers' Roles

There is a call for teachers to serve as leaders in the schools in new and different ways. No longer do teachers have to leave the classroom to have leadership responsibilities. As schools change, teachers and reading specialists can serve as leaders in curriculum and professional development efforts, in spearheading efforts to select materials or change reporting procedures, and so on. When teachers are offered and accept major responsibility and the power to make decisions, the commitment to follow through on implementation is greatly strengthened.

## Poor Solutions or Failed Reform

The lack of success of many school reform efforts in literacy can be attributed to a variety of reasons: ineffective, overly circumscribed solutions (e.g., a belief that one particular approach or program will create the changes in school performance), lackluster or poor implementation (e.g., the selection of effective approaches or programs, but little effort given to helping teachers learn how to implement the program in their classrooms), or lack of sustainability (e.g., too many new initiatives, with little time to learn one well). Moreover, problems in some schools are so complex that a single reform effort or initiative is not sufficient for improving student achievement.

## WHAT SHOULD WE DO?

Schools that have "beat the odds"—that is, they have done better than expected, given the demographics of the school population—provide some direction (and much inspiration) for us in our efforts to make large-scale changes in our schools. According to Taylor and colleagues (2002), "research on effective teachers and schools is surprisingly convergent" (p. 371). These schools employ teachers who have excellent classroom management skills and provide excellent literacy instruction, often involving small-group instruction for students. A sense of collaboration characterizes these schools as teachers work closely with reading specialists and other personnel, as well as with the parents of the students.

Alvermann (2002) noted:

> Effective literacy instruction for adolescents must take into account a host of factors, including students' perceptions of their competencies as readers and writers, their level of motivation and background knowledge, and their interests. To be effective, such instruction must be embedded in the regular curriculum and make use of multiple forms of texts read for multiple purposes in a variety of learning situations. (p. 203)

Alvermann's remarks are critical ones for reading specialists in middle or secondary schools. She calls for teachers, including reading specialists, to demonstrate sensitivity to the needs and interests of their adolescent students. Moreover, reading specialists are encouraged to work closely with content teachers to embed literacy into the regular curriculum.

We *can* improve literacy instruction in our schools. Reading specialists have an important role in this endeavor, not only in working with individual teachers but with groups of teachers. Information presented in Chapters 4, 5, and 6, provide important guidelines for such work. This chapter focuses on the school curriculum and how reading specialists in leadership roles can contribute to the development of the literacy curriculum.

## CURRICULUM DEVELOPMENT

Guidelines useful in thinking about a framework for a school reading program are presented below (Bean, 2002, pp. 4–6).

1. *Base goals and standards for reading on theory and research.* We hear much today about scientifically based reading research, and although there are areas of disagreement, there is much that we *do* know about reading instruction, especially beginning reading instruction.

Certainly, the work presented by the National Institute of Child Health and Human Development (2000), Snow and colleagues (1998) in *Preventing Reading Difficulties*, and the synthesis of studies in the *Handbook of Reading Research* (Kamil, Mosenthal, Pearson, & Barr, 2000) can be helpful resources for reading specialists as they work with teachers in curriculum development. Alverman's article (2002) on effective literacy programs for adolescents provides an important source for those interested in secondary schools, as does the information generated by the series of workshops on adolescent literacy held by the National Institute of Literacy, the National Institute of Child Health and Human Development, and the U.S. Department of Education (2003).

School personnel must, of course, be aware of the requirements of their specific states regarding reading instruction; and, if they are eligible for federal funding, they must be aware of the requirements of legislation for specific grants. Guidelines, standards, and requirements all provide a basis for discussion and for curriculum development or modification.

2. *Relate teacher beliefs and knowledge about reading instruction to research.* Reading specialists who work with teachers must not only gain a sense of what those teachers believe and know about reading instruction, they also must provide opportunities for teacher reflection and discussion about their beliefs. Teachers bring their own experiences, knowledge, and beliefs to the teaching of reading; they interpret research findings through different lenses. I am reminded of a teacher from a secondary background who had little knowledge about the importance of decoding instruction. Although the work in her graduate courses and experiences in primary classrooms convinced her that students did need to learn phonics, she still experienced much difficulty with other teachers who shared lessons that had little opportunity for students to read and write—to learn phonics within a meaningful context. Unless the reading specialist was aware of this individual's beliefs and knew how to help her work collaboratively with others in a group, problems could arise when she began to participate in curriculum development meetings.

---

*Think about This*

Think about the individual, described above, who must work with primary teachers who believe in a strong decoding program. What problems might arise? How could the beliefs and strengths of this individual be tapped in a way that improves reading instruction?

To develop a common understanding and terminology, teachers may be asked to read current articles about reading instruction that provide a springboard for discussion. These readings can also provide teachers with up-to-date information that will enable them to think more deeply about what they do in their classrooms and how it relates to what research indicates is best practice.

3. *Organize the curriculum framework so that it is usable.* Too often, curriculum plans sit on shelves or in teacher's desks, consulted only infrequently. Those involved in curriculum development must be certain to formulate plans that are coherent yet simple to use. It is essential that such plans provide a sequence of literacy instruction for K–12. With such a framework, teachers can gain a sense of "where in the curriculum various understandings, skills, and attitudes are addressed" (Bean, 2002, p. 6).

4. *Develop a process for change that involves all constituents.* According to Good (1973) in the *Dictionary of Education*, curriculum development is "a task of supervision directed towards designing or redesigning the guidelines for instruction, includes development of specifications indicating what is to be taught, by whom, when, where, and in what sequence or pattern" (p. 158). There are several important stages in curriculum development work. Described below are the initial stages that are important prerequisites to the actual development of curriculum (and to the later issues of implementation and evaluation).

## Stage 1

*What is the current situation in the school?* Before the current curriculum can be changed, it is essential to have a clear picture of what is occurring in the school and the level of the current knowledge about reading instruction. To gather this information requires consulting teachers about what they believe are the strengths and weaknesses of their current approaches. In addition, test data can be used to supply additional information about the effectiveness of the school's programs. Teachers may be interviewed, asked to complete questionnaires, or asked to participate in meetings to discuss their views about the reading program in their school.

One of the approaches to curriculum development is that of having teachers map the curriculum they are currently using. Jacobs (1997) described mapping as an activity that "enables teachers to show student work as it actually happens in the classroom and in relation to state or district standards" (p. 8) She lists seven steps in the mapping process. In the first step, teachers actually create a map of the three major elements of their curriculum—(1) content in terms of essential concepts and topics, (2) processes and skills, and (3) products and performances for assessment—using an agreed-upon form approved by the district. Jacobs suggested that teachers use the calendar as a basic guide for compiling the form, recording what they actually do in their classrooms. The remaining steps in her procedure consist of efforts to share what is being taught at the various grade levels and across grade levels and to make decisions about what needs to be reviewed and revised. This effort can certainly constitute a long-range professional development project for teachers. Teachers are often surprised by the repetition that occurs across grades or the fact that some things are not taught at all!

This mapping procedure can be used by reading specialists as a means of developing teachers' awareness of what is taught at each grade level; it can also generate topics for discussion that can be extremely helpful in developing the literacy curriculum and making modifications in instructional practices. Figure 7.1 provides a partial example of one such form.

The leader of the curriculum development effort, in collaboration with others, must decide how to approach the actual change process:

Will all teachers be involved or a representative few?
If not all are involved, how can others be consulted and informed?
What is the time line for the process?
What are the goals and outcomes of the effort?

## Stage 2

*What can we learn from research and theory?* Information from books and journal articles should be shared with teachers; outside experts may be consulted so that all have a sense of current knowledge and theory about reading instruction. Often, districts invite an expert to address all teachers or a representative committee; this event should be followed by opportunities for discussion and debate about the issues presented. At this point, as well as in later stages, teachers' beliefs, attitudes, and ideas

| Month | Skills/strategies | Content used | Assessment |
|---|---|---|---|
| September | Review of consonants (initial and ending) Introduce short vowels Finding main idea | Basal Stories 1–4 | Worksheets Unit test Fluency checks |
| October | Short vowels Summarizing | Basal Stories 5–8 Selected trade book | Worksheets Pseudo words Journal responses to each chapter in book |

FIGURE 7.1. Map of second-grade reading instruction (partial).

must be taken into consideration and opportunities for discussion about differences provided.

## Stage 3

*What constitutes a coherent, usable curriculum plan?* Armed with knowledge of the curriculum used in the school and a solid understanding of the current research about literacy instruction, the group or groups responsible for curriculum development can begin to struggle with the content and format of the plan, investigating what structure can best be used by the classroom teachers. This stage offers a wonderful opportunity for teachers across the grades (K–12) to begin to communicate with each other so that the developed plan contains an articulated, sequential identification of skills, strategies, understandings, and knowledge. During this stage, drafts of plans should be shared with those not working on this effort and requests for feedback included.

Au (2001) describes one procedure for guiding change in a school. Teachers are asked to describe a shared vision of what excellent readers can do when they leave that elementary school. Then teachers at each grade level are asked to identify the special contributions they make to the fulfillment of that vision. She asks teachers to set benchmarks in three areas: attitudes, comprehension, and strategies and skills. When there is agreement, teachers then make certain that alignment exists between their statements and standards of what they must achieve. Finally, teachers develop assessment measures that help them determine whether they have met the agreed upon benchmarks. This process is one that requires time for discussion and interaction among the faculty at the school.

### Stage 4

*How should the plan be shared with others? What implementation strategies are necessary?* Too often, it is the implementation stage that falls short of the goal. Those who have worked on the development of the plan are committed to it—and perhaps use it. Others, if they do not understand the plan and how it works, may just ignore it or implement it halfheartedly. If teachers have been involved during the entire process, they are more likely to accept and use the plan. Therefore, it is important to keep all teachers apprised during each stage and to seek their input.

## SELECTION OF MATERIALS

Teachers frequently make decisions about classroom instruction based on the anthologies or basals that they are using in their classroom. In fact, researchers (Fawson & Reutzel, 2000; Hoffman et al., 1998) have reported that such materials are still the most significant component of literacy instruction. And, given that specific materials, once selected, become the driving force for at least 5 or more years, careful attention must be given to selecting materials so that they fit with the objectives, goals, and standards that have been formulated by the district. Too often the materials selected become the curriculum guide or plan for the district.

### Guidelines for Selecting Basals

Once the district has decided that it is going to adopt a specific series as a means of providing a core reading program, literacy personnel need to think about both content and process issues. Both are important.

### Process

The process to be used is extremely important because it often involves more than professional issues. Publishers are eager to obtain adoptions; school districts need to be certain that they abide by the same guidelines or rules for all materials being considered. What selection procedure should be used? Will all teachers, or a representative group, serve on the committee? What are the rules? If publishers are invited to present their "wares," how much time do they get and what can they "give" or provide to teachers? Will the district decide upon piloting the materials (a common practice)?

A careful consideration of the process reduces the possibility that the outcome will be met by accusations of unfairness or bias in materials selection. Most districts try to select a committee that includes a representative group of teachers and administrators. All grade levels in which materials will be used should be represented; so should all schools in a district. At the same time, it would be wise to include parents; they provide a unique perspective as well as generate the community support needed to approve the final decision. Students may also be included on the committee, especially if the materials to be selected apply to the upper levels.

## Content

The following guidelines can be useful in thinking about which basal or anthology to select.

1. *Review the philosophy.* Before proceeding with a review of materials, spend time reviewing or developing the philosophy or goals of the district. In that way, materials can be selected that match the goals of the school, thereby reducing the possibility that the scope and sequence of the basal will become the curriculum of the school.

2. *Conduct a needs assessment of teachers in the district.* A short questionnaire or brief talks with all teachers can generate a list of priorities. Often, teachers have specific concerns about current materials and their inability to meet the needs of the children. Time spent obtaining ideas about what the group thinks is important and usually means there will be less dissension later.

3. *Plan for a research update.* Make certain that the committee knows what is current in the field. An expert can be invited to make a presentation; the group can be given materials to read. Both should be followed by group discussion. A resolution of the International Reading Association Board, titled "Buyer Be Wary" (May 2002), discusses the need for those involved in selecting materials to be especially cautious in their deliberations. This document encourages program reviewers to look closely at the publishers' claims in relation to program effectiveness.

4. *Decide upon the "ideal."* What should the final material look like? What should it include? By designing a checklist, or modifying an existing one, the group can more efficiently review materials. Various

checklists are available, such as those developed by Lapp, Fisher, Flood, Goss-Moore, and Moore (2002) and Simmons and Kame'enui (2002). Most of the checklists include a review of content, the teachers' manual, the scope and sequence of skills, the supplemental material (including workbooks), and assessment procedures.

5. *Review materials.* The committee can quickly screen and discard those basals that do not appear to meet the identified criteria. Then an in-depth review must be made of the three or four that appear to be acceptable. The committee can decide to break into smaller groups to review specific texts and present findings to the entire group, or everyone in the group may review all texts. The group may decide to track the teaching of a specific strategy or skill through the grade levels, to determine how the strategy is taught at each level. For example, committee members could focus on how students are taught to summarize from the early grades through grade 8.

Teachers, of course, are interested in the readability of the text. Although readability formulas can be used, such estimates are subjective and should be used cautiously. Schumm and Mangrum (1991) have developed a strategy, known as FLIP (framework for fostering textbook thinking) that helps those in middle grades conduct an evaluation of text difficulty.

6. *Make a final decision.* In addition to using information from in-depth reviews, the committee may talk with teachers in other districts who are using the materials to get their perspectives. At this stage, the committee should come to a consensus, or if necessary, vote to make a decision about the text to be selected. It is, of course, much better if the group can agree on the "best" basal, but this may not be possible. If no clear-cut decision emerges, more time may need to be spent in analyzing the available materials.

## TECHNOLOGY IN THE READING PROGRAM

Teachers in today's schools need to be competent users of technology, employing it as a tool to enhance the literacy program in their classrooms. Indeed, technology is fast becoming an integral part of every classroom. According to Cattagni and Farris (2001), 77% of U.S. classrooms have Internet connections, and it is expected that almost all classrooms will have Internet-connected computers within several years. Teachers need many skills to use electronic technology effectively:

locating resources about literacy on the Internet, communicating with others using technology, entering, accessing, and interpreting data about students and their accomplishments, and becoming knowledgeable about the various software programs that can be used to deliver instruction to students.

McVee and Dickson (2002) noted that the issues of technology and related responsibilities may make teachers feel like Sisyphus—"that unfortunate citizen of Greece who was sentenced to an eternity of pushing a rock up a steep hill only to have it roll down again and again" (p. 635). They developed a rubric as a guide for reviewing software for programs designed for use in K–3 classrooms. The rubric identifies the following questions as ones that can be used for reviewing software:

1. What observations can we make about overall media presentation?
2. How easy is the software to navigate?
3. Does the software change over time? With each use? With prolonged interactions? Multiple uses?
4. Which types of assessments are built into the program? How important or useful are these for users and teachers?
5. How closely do activities fit classroom needs? Are they interesting? Educational? Fun?
6. How would we rate the overall value of the software? Would this be a good investment for my classroom?
7. How compatible is this software with an emergent literacy approach that integrates reading, writing, listening, and speaking? (McVee & Dickson, 2002, p. 639)

These questions can be adapted for use at other grade levels. One resource that can be used by schools to heighten awareness of what is needed in the area of technology is the National Educational Technology Standards for Students: Connecting Curriculum and Technology (International Society for Technology in Education, 2000). This guide identifies standards at all levels for both preservice teachers and pre-K–12 students.

## KNOWLEDGE AND UNDERSTANDING OF STATE AND FEDERAL REQUIREMENTS

Every district, regardless of student demographics, location, or size, has requirements that it must meet to comply with state legislation on curriculum, assessment, and instruction matters. Most states have developed standards that students must meet; therefore, schools must use those standards in developing their literacy curriculum. Furthermore, any district eligible for Title 1 services must, of course, develop a plan that addresses the requirements in state and federal legislation; issues such as eligibility, accountability, models for instruction, inclusion of parent involvement programs, and so on, may all need to be described in the district plan. Moreover, there may be potential funding programs that require reading specialists or others in the district to write a proposal that enables them to receive that funding. For example, Reading First legislation (as part of the No Child Left Behind legislation) at the federal level required states to apply for funding by writing a proposal that described their plan for implementing Reading First programs. The state application was then reviewed by an expert panel at the federal level; once approved, eligible school districts in that state were invited to submit their own plans for implementing Reading First in their districts. Generally, schools assigned teams to write those plans.

Such opportunities offer the possibility of receiving increased funding for improving reading instruction; at the same time, they require that reading specialists (1) become knowledgeable about the requirements of the legislation, (2) are able to write a coherent plan that addresses the requirements, and (3) are able to work with others so that the contents of the plan are consistent with what is required, and at the same time, reflect the goals, practices, and beliefs of the district and its educators. (Chapter 10 provides information that may be helpful to reading specialists who have direct responsibility for writing proposals to receive state or federal funding.) In the following sections, the role of reading specialists in relation to various state and federal initiatives is discussed. As part of this discussion, there is a section that describes the No Child Left Behind (NCLB) legislation, and its accompanying Reading First grant program.

## IMPACT OF FEDERAL OR STATE INITIATIVES ON THE ROLE OF READING SPECIALISTS

Reading specialists in all schools must keep up to date about various governmental regulations and legislation. State or federal government agencies send information to school officials and sometimes invite one or more educators from a district to attend informational meetings in which specific initiatives are discussed. Conferences held by the state, local educational support agencies, or professional groups typically offer sessions in which such legislation is described. Information can also be obtained from the state or federal websites on which various legislative actions are described or summarized. The website of the International Reading Association (i.e., *www.reading.org*) also provides useful information. The information below about the NCLB legislation and Reading First comes from the federal government's website *http://www.nclb.gov/next/overview/index.html*.

## No Child Left Behind (NCLB)

The NCLB law, according to the website, represents the most sweeping changes to the Elementary and Secondary Education Act (ESEA) since it was enacted in 1965. The legislation has an impact on education in grades K–12 and is based upon four basic principles: strong accountability, local control and flexibility, an increased role for parents, and scientifically based reading research. As part of this legislation, Title 1 received the largest funding increase in its history, with annual expenditures totaling more than $10 billion (Borman, 2002–2003).

As part of the accountability effort, each state must develop a set of standards for what children should know and be able to do in various areas, including reading. Then all students must be tested, using assessment measures that are aligned with the standards. By 2005–2006, tests must be administered in grades 3–8 in reading. Schools are expected to make adequate yearly progress (AYP). Results will be disaggregated to determine the growth of various groups, including those who are economically disadvantaged, those from racial or ethnic minority groups, those with learning disabilities, and those with limited English proficiency. If progress is inadequate, schools will be held accountable—that is, low-scoring schools will be penalized. NCLB affects all public schools in this country, K–12; therefore, reading specialists at all levels need to be familiar with it and the implications it has for students and their teachers.

## Reading First

As part of the NCLB legislation, education dollars will be distributed to states with approved proposals; the goal of the program is to improve reading instruction for K–3 students and ensure that children learn to read well by the end of third grade. Reading First funds are designated for districts in which there are large numbers of students living in poverty and in which there is low achievement. As mentioned previously, state applications were reviewed by an expert panel; once approved, eligible districts were invited to submit their plans for review at the state level. Plans were required to specify how districts would address the following areas:

- Developing a reading program that was based on scientifically sound reading research and that would teach all students to read at or above grade level no later than the end of grade 3.
- District procedures used for providing professional development and other support to K–3 teachers (and special education teachers K–12), so that they can teach students to read more effectively.
- The assessment measures—outcome, screening, diagnostic, and classroom based—allocated to determine students' strengths and needs.
- The materials proposed to implement the essential components of reading instruction.
- The procedures proposed to strengthen coordination among schools, early literacy programs, and family literacy programs.

The legislation defines scientifically based reading research as "research that applies rigorous, systematic, and objective procedures to obtain valid knowledge relevant to reading development, reading instruction, and reading difficulties" (No Child Left Behind Act of 2001, Sec. 1208). The International Reading Association has a position statement ("What is Evidence-Based Reading Research," 2002b) that provides a clear definition and a number of resources for those interested in learning more about this topic. In that statement, scientifically based research is defined as follows:

*Objective.* Data obtained in the research would be identified and interpreted in a similar manner by any reader.

*Valid.* The data represent tasks that are relevant to reading, that is, that children need to accomplish to be successful readers

*Reliable.* Data will be the same regardless of who collects them or when they are collected.

*Systematic.* There is a rigorous research design (in the Reading First legislation, this means either experimentation or observation).

*Refereed.* The research has appeared in a peer-reviewed journal, which indicates that it has been approved for publication by other researchers or scholars.

Research that provides the strongest designs for demonstrating effectiveness are those that are experimental—that is, those in which results from a specific practice or approach are compared to a control group, with random assignment to the groups. Quasi-experimental designs are often used in education because of the difficulty or inappropriateness of random assignment. In this case, random assignment is not used, but various statistical procedures are used to control for any selected preexisting differences in the groups. Experts also agree that there must be a convergence of information from a number of studies before any single finding is accepted as conclusive.

Another aspect of the focus on scientifically based research is that districts are being asked to select and use materials or reading programs that are based on such research. Doing so is a difficult task because few studies of large reading programs can be defined as scientifically based. Often districts justify the use of specific materials by analyzing the research that undergirds the instructional processes for specific reading elements within those programs. For example, a school district may analyze a large basal program to determine whether it presents phonics instruction in a manner found to be effective through scientifically based research. Specifically, is phonics taught in a systematic and explicit manner (National Reading Panel Report, 2000)? As mentioned previously in this chapter, various checklists are available that can be used to review such comprehensive reading materials.

Various chapters in this book provide information that can be helpful to those involved in developing or implementing Reading First programs. Assessment outcomes are an important part of Reading First; students and their performance must be monitored on a regular basis, and there must be provision for diagnostic assessment if students are not progressing as expected. (See Chapter 8 for more information about assessment; Chapter 9, for information about parent involvement and family literacy, another component of Reading First; and Chapter 6 for the professional development aspect of Reading First.)

Useful resources for those wanting to learn more about NCLB and Reading First include the National Reading Panel report (National Institute of Child Health and Human Development, 2000); Snow and colleagues (1998); Center for the Improvement of Early Reading Achievement (1998); Kamil and colleagues (2000); Neuman and Dickinson

(2001); and International Reading Association (2002b; includes articles from *The Reading Teacher* that describe instructional practices consistent with the National Reading Panel findings).

## SUMMARY

In this chapter, problems associated with creating change in schools are discussed to provide a backdrop to the issue of developing a school reading program. Guidelines for developing a school reading program are presented and processes for creating change elaborated, highlighting the importance of involving as many teachers as possible in the curriculum development process. This is followed by a discussion of materials selection that emphasizes the need for establishing criteria with which to analyze the materials. There is also a discussion about the importance of technology and the resources that enhance knowledge of this aspect of a reading program. Finally, there is a section that describes basic elements of the No Child Left Behind and Reading First legislation.

### Reflections

1. Think about the problems associated with large-scale change described earlier in this chapter as they relate to a school with which you are familiar. Does the school you are thinking about have any of those problems? Others?
2. Meet with several colleagues to talk about your vision of what an excellent reader (at the end of sixth grade) can do. Discuss your views with each other. How similar are they? Different?

### Activities

1. If you are a classroom teacher, try to map your reading curriculum for the entire year. Use that map to think about whether the curriculum helps you accomplish the goals that you think are important for your students.
2. Use the criteria from one of the suggested frameworks to evaluate a set of basal materials. Compare your evaluation with a colleague's.

# 8

## Assessment

"I taught my dog to speak."
"I don't hear him speaking."
"I didn't say he learned it."

Assessment helps us determine the difference between *teaching* and *learning*. The term *assessment* generates much emotion in today's schools. There are those who believe that the emphasis on assessment is an important means of improving instruction; others believe that we put too much emphasis on assessment, thereby narrowing the curriculum and reducing teacher creativity. In reality, assessment is an important aspect of the total school reading program and one that must be planned and implemented as carefully as the curriculum and instructional plans for the schools.

## WHAT, WHY, AND FOR WHOM?

The terms *assessment* and *tests* are often confused. Assessment is the task of gathering data on which to base evaluative or judgment-oriented decisions. Such data are multidimensional, encompassing more than

137

just standardized tests. They range from observations and interviews to informal tasks and performance measures, such as writing a retell or responding to a selection. Glazer (1998), in fact, states that "Assessment is instruction." Even as they are teaching a lesson, teachers often modify or adapt what they are doing, based on their informal assessment of whether students are "getting it."

Assessment measures are necessary for a number of reasons, and they are relevant to many different audiences. Certainly, the school administration and the community (including parents and taxpayers) are interested in whether their schools are performing satisfactorily. In this case, assessment measures serve as an *outcome* or accountability tool. The measure used is frequently a norm-referenced test that compares students from a specific district or school with others like them. Such information can be helpful to the school in determining in which areas their program is strong (e.g., students do well in reading vocabulary) and in which areas they might need to improve (e.g., comprehension scores are weak).

Assessment measures can also be used to inform parents about their children—what they do well, and where they may need to improve. Parents often receive various types of information, ranging from their children's scores on standardized tests to much more specific feedback gathered by the classroom teacher. The results presented by the classroom teacher tend to be far more tailored to the individual and, more frequently, related closely to the instructional program used. Thus the classroom teacher shares with parents the results of unit tests from the basal, running records or informal inventories, and even worksheets that have been completed by the children.

Those who are responsible for teaching students also need to know the results of various assessment measures. *Diagnostic* assessment assists teachers in making decisions about instruction and in pinpointing possible areas to address if a student is experiencing difficulty. Closely related to these diagnostic measures are *monitoring* measures that help determine whether students have shown progress over time. Such measures might include recognition of sight words, fluency checks, or changes in writing. These measures can be very helpful tools for teachers, who can then decide whether there is a need for additional support, a change in instructional practice, or some other diagnostic assessment to obtain more information about a child's performance.

There are also measures that serve as *initial screening* tools, assisting teachers in planning their curriculum and instruction. These measures are often used by reading specialists at the beginning of the year to provide baseline information about students and to make decisions about which children are eligible for special services.

These four types of measures—outcome, diagnostic, monitoring, and initial screening measures—serve different purposes and require different types of assessment tools. It is the outcome measure that has generated the most controversy, because it is often related to some sort of punitive/reward system. At least 44 states have what is called "high-stakes assessment," that is, tests that are used to make major decisions about students (e.g., whether they can matriculate to the next grade, the form of diploma they will get, etc.). High-stakes assessments are also used by the state or federal government to make decisions about whether schools are identified as "low-scoring" schools that need to make major improvements in their instructional performance.

In this chapter, I highlight information about assessment that is critical to reading specialists and their responsibilities. In today's schools, especially with the passage of the No Child Left Behind legislation, reading specialists must be aware of the advantages and limitations of many different types of assessment measures. They must be able to administer and interpret these measures, and they must understand how to share their interpretations with classroom teachers, parents, administrators, and others in the community.

## PRINCIPLES OF ASSESSMENT

1. *Facilitate a match between instruction and assessment.* In selecting assessment measures, especially outcome measures, careful attention must be given to the match between the instruction provided in the school and the measure chosen. Tests need to be selected that match the objectives and curriculum of the school. Teachers often bemoan the fact that students are tested on some skill that is not introduced in the curriculum until the following grade level! There is strong evidence that the closer the overlap between curriculum and test items, the better students will perform; this just makes sense. This is not to say that teachers should be teaching to the test, but it is foolish to ignore the demands of a test that students will be taking as a measure of their achievement. At times, this outcome measure is a test developed by the state, based on standards that have been adopted by that state. In that case, it again makes sense for reading specialists and their colleagues to work to-

gether to decide how and what the schools are teaching so that students can achieve those standards. Only then will the outcome measure be a fair assessment of students' performance. Beresik and Bean (2002), in their study of teachers' perceptions about a state assessment test, found that teachers did not feel as though they had received sufficient professional development that would help them implement instruction that addressed state standards as measured by that outcome test. This complaint was especially common among teachers who taught at grade levels below the level at which the test was administered.

2. *Develop or select assessment measures for major components of literacy K–12.* At all levels (i.e., primary, intermediate, middle school, and secondary), reading specialists and their colleagues must make decisions about which components of literacy to assess. In the primary grades, assessment measures should focus more on basic skills as well as comprehension and writing. In the upper grades, more emphasis is placed on comprehension, vocabulary, and writing. The key is for school personnel to select instruments that reflect a logical and realistic progression from level to level and across all of the components.

3. *Develop a system of literacy assessment that reflects the goals of the school and use assessment tools that are reliable, valid, and practical to administer.* Too often, there is no agreed-upon system of literacy assessment in the school community. Many different tools are used by school personnel, some of which are disparate with school goals. Other assessment tools may be so complicated that they are not usable by the classroom teacher; they may also take so much time for administration that valuable instructional time is lost. Furthermore, published instruments may be selected that are not technically valid or reliable; instruments developed by districts themselves can also lack such technical sophistication. For example, if a school decides to assess students' written retelling of a story, careful attention must be given to the rubric used to score this retelling so that there is *reliability* or consistency in the scoring of that instrument. Otherwise, little use can be made of the scores. Also, the tools employed must be *valid*—that is, they actually measure what they purport to measure. For example, a spelling test is not a measure of composition skill, although spelling, as part of a conventions rubric, could be used as one indicator of performance in composition.

Assessment tools should be usable by the teachers who administer them, whether they are reading specialists or classroom teachers. If teachers see these assessments as a burden that only take time away from the instructional program, and if they are not provided with the training they need to see the value of these measures, there will be little value in administering them.

4. *Teachers need assistance in applying data to instructional decision making.* There is clear evidence that when teachers use data to make instructional decisions, student performance improves. Yet, too often, instruction in the classroom is "activity" or materials based; that is, decisions about instruction are based on the selection that comes next in the book. One of the important roles of the reading specialist is to help teachers make decisions about their instruction, based on the results of the students in their classroom. Figure 8.1 lists scores of students in one third-grade classroom on several literacy assessment measures. In the vignette below, I describe the work of the reading specialist as she helps the teacher make sense of the results.

Samantha Jones, the reading specialist, and Roberta Reed, the third-grade teacher, were reviewing the scores of some of Roberta's students on the initial screening measures given at the beginning of the year. It was obvious to them that students were doing fairly well with basic sight words; almost all students scored 75% or better. Students were not performing as well on the pseudo-word test, with 11 of them getting less than 75% correct. Many students also were experiencing difficulty with fluent oral reading (reading below 80 correct words per minute). The poor scores on the retelling were also of concern, and students had some difficulty responding to questions after reading. Roberta and Samantha identified two students (Sally and Henry) about whom they had serious concerns.

Samantha and Roberta made the following decisions after a lengthy discussion. First, all students in third grade would benefit from activities that emphasized fluency or practice, and Samantha shared with Roberta various ways to facilitate both (e.g., repeated readings, choral reading, etc.) Samantha indicated that she would come into the room 4 days a week to work on decoding with the 11 students who seemed to have the most difficulty; she told Roberta that she would emphasize word building or manipulation activities to help students apply what they knew about letter–sound matches to identifying new words. All lessons would include opportunities for reading connected text.

Because of the low retelling score, both educators agreed that students did not seem to understand the task of retelling and that the entire group would benefit from lessons that helped them understand (1) the activity of retelling and why it would help them remember a story, and (2) strategies to help them think about re-

Teacher name (last): _____ Grade _3_

| Student name | Pseudo-word | Sight word | Fluency | | Comprehension | |
|---|---|---|---|---|---|---|
| | % | % | Words read | Words correct | Retell n/55 | Question n/8 |
| Frank | 60 | 89 | 52 | 44 | 7 | 3 |
| Juan | 55 | 93 | 90 | 86 | 6 | 6 |
| Clyde | 85 | 97 | 90 | 87 | 10 | 5 |
| Melissa | 45 | 93 | 102 | 98 | 13 | 5 |
| Cindy | 60 | 95 | 57 | 53 | 13 | 6 |
| Sally | 35 | 76 | 25 | 11 | 0 | 4 |
| Bob | 90 | 97 | 87 | 83 | 19 | 6 |
| Jerome | 90 | 98 | 143 | 143 | 11 | 8 |
| Ralph | 95 | 82 | 52 | 48 | 14 | 5 |
| Gail | 80 | 96 | 102 | 99 | 7 | 8 |
| Celeste | 20 | 95 | 57 | 52 | 11 | 4 |
| Joseph | 25 | 98 | 65 | 61 | 30 | 7 |
| Tyrone | 25 | 96 | 63 | 59 | 26 | 6 |
| Henry | 45 | 67 | 29 | 18 | 15 | 5 |
| Mark | 60 | 92 | 81 | 77 | 19 | 6 |
| Julie | 40 | 93 | 75 | 71 | 8 | 6 |

FIGURE 8.1. Example of a student data collection sheet, third grade, pretests.

telling, such as story structure or story mapping. They would also be given opportunities to retell orally as well as in writing. Samantha and Roberta knew that they would need to give serious thought to how to build the comprehension skills of these students, given that there would be much more emphasis on reading more challenging and conceptually difficult text in third grade. However, at this point, they decided to begin with a focus on retelling.

Samantha told Roberta that she would do some additional diagnostic testing on Sally and Henry to get a better idea of their specific problems. She decided to administer an informal reading inventory to see how they responded to different genres of text at varying levels. She also thought it would be helpful to gather data on their phonological abilities and writing skills. Furthermore, she suggested to Roberta that it would be a good idea for the two of them to analyze the writing abilities of all the students within the next month. Roberta and Samantha agreed to meet in 1 month to talk about their instruction and to make adjustments, as needed.

This vignette provides a description of how one reading specialist worked collaboratively with a classroom teacher in using test results to make instructional decisions.

5. *Opportunity for student self-assessment and reflection should be built into the program.* Although assessment and accountability are major concerns in schools today, unfortunately, there is less consideration given to the importance of *self*-assessment by the students. Nevertheless, there is strong support for involving students in the process of evaluating their own work (Hansen, 1998; Weber, 1999). Such self-assessment should enable students to make some decisions about their own learning. In fact, Tierney, Johnston, Moore, and Valencia (2000) predicted the continuation of an increased emphasis on learner-centered assessment that signifies "a shift in why assessments are pursued as well as how and who pursues them" (p. 244).

The use of rubrics in classrooms can promote such self-evaluation. A rubric is a scoring guide, with criteria, for judging the relative quality of assessment products. Figure 8.2 shows a sample rubric for assessing readers' responses to a passage (Grade 3 Reading Assessment Test in Pennsylvania, preliminary version, September 2002). Figure 8.3 is the student version of that rubric, which teachers can use to help students become knowledgeable about the demands of the task and to become familiar with assessing their own work.

Portfolio assessment also can be used as a means of promoting ownership of work. Such assessment can begin in the early grades with the collection of student work, writing samples, reading attitude forms, and books read, and progress to more complicated portfolios created at the middle and high school levels.

## ISSUES IN ASSESSMENT

### Who Should Be Involved in Developing the Assessment Plan?

Although assessment plans can be developed by an individual or a small group of administrators, it is best that such a plan be developed by a team or committee, including teachers, reading specialists, department chairs, principals, and parent representatives. Such a team, led by an administrator knowledgeable about tests and assessments, can deal with the issues that generally face such groups:

*Level 4*

- *Demonstrates a thorough understanding of the text. There are no errors in text-based information.*
- *Makes strong integrated connections among ideas within and beyond the text.*
- *Addresses all aspects of the task.*

*Level 3*

- *Demonstrates an adequate understanding of the text. There are no major errors in text-based information.*
- *Makes connections among ideas within and adds additional idea(s) from beyond the text.*
- *Substantially addresses the task.*

*Level 2*

- *Demonstrates a partial understanding of the text. There may be errors in text-based information.*
- *The response makes connections among ideas within the text (retelling).*
- *Partially addresses the task.*

*Level 1*

- *Demonstrates very limited understanding of the text. There may be many errors in text-based information.*
- *The response makes few or no connections among ideas within the text.*
- *Minimally addresses the task.*

*Level 0*

- *Paper is blank.*
- *The paper is illegible or incomprehensible.*
- *The response has no relationship to the task.*

**FIGURE 8.2.** Pennsylvania Department of Education Grade 3 Reading Assessment Rubric—Scorer Language; preliminary version, January 2002.

> Which assessments best match the curriculum in our schools, K–12?
> Which assessments are required by the state?
> How can we get the best information with the least amount of disruption to the instructional schedule?
> What training is necessary if teachers are to be able to administer, score (if necessary), and use the results?

Too often, decisions about assessment are made in isolation, with changes occurring at one or another level, precluding the possibility of

*Level 4*

*In my answer:*
- *I show I understand the whole passage, and I have all of the information right.*
- *I make strong connections among ideas in the passage and my own ideas.*
- *I write about all parts of the task.*

*Level 3*

*In my answer:*
- *I show I understand the passage, and I have the important information right.*
- *I connect ideas in the passage with each other and add my own ideas.*
- *I write about the task.*

*Level 2*

*In my answer:*
- *I show I understand part of the passage, but I may make some mistakes about the information.*
- *I connect ideas in the passage with each other through a retelling.*
- *I write about some parts of the task.*

*Level 1*

*In my answer:*
- *I show I tried to understand the passage, but I make many mistakes about the information.*
- *I just write some words about the passage.*
- *I write about few parts of the task.*

*Level 0*

- *I left my paper blank.*
- *My paper was too hard for other people to read.*
- *I didn't write about the task.*

FIGURE 8.3. Pennsylvania Department of Education Grade 3 Reading Assessment Rubric—Student Language; preliminary version, January 2002.

continuity. And too often, districts cannot use their assessment tools to make decisions because they have (1) changed them too frequently, or (2) the measures are not comparable from one level to another.

School personnel should be familiar with the assessment tools being used by the district and able to discuss and communicate the results of such assessments to parents and others in the community interested in the work of the school. The emphasis by the federal government (in the NCLB legislation) on assessment results and accountability certainly makes it imperative that schools be able to explain not only *what* they are doing but *how well* they are doing!

## How Are Assessment Results Reported?

Again, reading specialists may find it necessary to assist in developing ways that schools report assessment results. They themselves may also be responsible for such reporting. Different audiences are interested in these results: teachers, students, district administration, parents, and community members (including those on the school board). The school district should have an established means of reporting students' scores to each teacher; such reports may be similar to the one in Figure 8.1. The reading specialist should be available to assist the teacher in interpreting and using the results for instructional decision making. The reading specialist may also assist the teacher in deciding how scores of individual students can best be reported and explained to parents or to students themselves. Building principals need to receive reports in many different forms: by class, grade level, and domain or area (e.g., reading comprehension, fluency, etc.), to cite a few. They may wish to have data disaggregated by ethnic group, socioeconomic status, or special education eligibility. Again, the reading specialist may work with the principal on interpreting the results of the literacy assessment; adjustments in the instruction or curriculum may be indicated. The reading specialist and principal together may decide to make a presentation about test results to the entire faculty.

Reporting to parents is certainly a key responsibility of the schools. Reading specialists should, of course, be aware of the ways by which literacy performance is reported and what the specific scores mean: letter grades, effort scores, grade-level reporting. In addition, they should be able to interpret those results to parents, especially parents of struggling readers. It is probable that those parents may want to meet with the reading specialist to discuss their children's scores.

Although not all reading specialists will have the responsibility for interpreting assessment results to the school board or community, including the media, some may. It is essential that the district be proactive in sharing assessment results. Not only should results be shared, but information should be given so that interested stakeholders understand what the school is doing to improve students' achievement.


## What Are the Limitations of Standardized Tests?

Reading specialists, because they frequently make use of tests in their work, need to be especially aware of the limitations of those tests, especially those that are high stake or have the potential to label or affect students' lives in a detrimental manner. Two limitations are discussed here. First, a test is a *sample* of all questions that can be asked about a subject and, in addition, a *sample* of a students' performance at a single point in time. Therefore, although test companies work to ensure that the items selected constitute a representative sample of important knowledge and skills, the fact remains that some students might have done better if a different sample of equally adequate questions had been used on the test. Furthermore, on any given day, an external factor such as illness or a disagreement with a parent may have affected a student's performance.

Second, changes in the schools' scores can be caused by changes in student population. If a school is one whose population demonstrates high mobility or attrition, then there can be significant differences in the population that takes the test from one administration date to another. Some students may not have been in the school for more than 2 or 3 months. In fact, Kane and Staiger in Kober (2002) estimated that more than 70% of the year-to-year variations in average test scores for a given school or grade could be attributed to external factors rather than educational factors. Reading specialists need to be aware of how assessment can help inform teachers and others; at the same time, they need to have an excellent understanding of the limitations of tests and how their results can be misused.

## SUMMARY

Assessment is an important responsibility of the reading specialist, not only for assessing the strengths and needs of individual students but also for making decisions about the performance of classes, schools, and the district as a whole. Assessment should be closely related to instruction, and there should be a sequential, comprehensive assessment system, K–12. In addition, various stakeholders, including teachers and community representatives, should be involved in making decisions about the assessment of literacy. Multiple assessment measures that display established technical adequacy should be used. Reading specialists may have responsibility for working with teachers, administrators, and the community interpreting and applying the results of assessment.

## Reflections

What are the strengths and weaknesses of various assessment instruments with which you are familiar?

## Activities

1. Interview a reading specialist in a district about his or her role in assessment. Which assessment tools does he or she use? Does the district have a plan of assessment, K–12? How does the assessment differ from level to level?
2. Select an assessment tool used by a district with which you are familiar and investigate whether the instrument meets a standard of technical adequacy.

# 9

## School, Community, and Family Partnerships

It takes a village to raise a child.
—AFRICAN PROVERB

Although this expression is often used (perhaps, *too* frequently), its merit cannot be disputed. When teachers are asked to identify their greatest problem in working with struggling readers, they often mention the lack of parental involvement in providing additional support or attending to the child's behavioral needs, especially in schools where there are large numbers of students from poor or minority backgrounds (National Center for Educational Statistics, 1998). Teachers in the early grades decry the fact that students come to kindergarten without the background knowledge/exposure that enables them to learn to read; these teachers are concerned that children do not have the literacy and language experiences that provide the foundation for learning to read.

In the past, some educators believed that it was their job to teach and that parents had the responsibility of "parenting." This viewpoint

149

has certainly changed; the education of the child is one that requires the effort of both. The research evidence is clear. When there is parental involvement and support, students have a much better chance of success in school (Henderson & Berla, 1995). When parents are involved in their children's schooling, the children earn higher grades and test scores, and they stay in school longer. In addition, the increased pressure on educators to account for levels of student achievement has generated a need for more parental involvement. In its No Child Left Behind legislation, the federal government gave parents a range of options to pursue if their children are placed in unsuccessful schools. Schools must have supplemental programs for children with special needs, and parents have the choice of transferring their children to better-performing public schools. Whether we agree with this policy or feel that it puts the focus of success solely on schools and teachers, the fact is that all schools and all teachers must think about their involvement in the community in new and different ways.

Epstein's (1995) research-based framework includes six types of parental involvement:

1. Parenting: helping families establish home environments that support children's development.
2. Communicating: designing and using effective forms of communication about programs and children's growth.
3. Volunteering: recruiting and organizing help and support in schools.
4. Learning at home: providing information and ideas to families about how to help students.
5. Decision making: including parents in school decisions.
6. Collaboration with the community.

Reading specialists and their colleagues can implement many different efforts to foster growth in these areas.

This chapter discusses the reading specialist's involvement with community agencies and institutions, addressing Epstein's (1995) sixth point of collaborating with the community. Guidelines for working with volunteers and paraprofessionals in the schools are provided. Lastly, the role of the reading specialist in working with families and addressing issues of parenting, communicating, learning at home, and decision making is explored.

# INVOLVEMENT WITH COMMUNITY AGENCIES

There are many different agencies with which reading specialists might work; involvement with five important entities is discussed here: preschool providers, libraries, community-based programs, universities, and volunteer and paraprofessional groups.

## Preschool Providers

The 5-year-olds who enter kindergartens come with a variety of experiences, many of them having attended day-care centers, nursery, or preschools. Some arrive having learned not only school and learning behaviors but also literacy skills that enable them to move comfortably into the kindergarten setting. Others seem to struggle with literacy tasks. Research on the cognitive development of young children emphasizes the importance of high-quality early learning experiences. There is evidence of great variability in the quality of the preschool experiences that children receive, especially in preschool programs serving children from poor families (Snow et al., 1998). At the same time, the quality of child-care programs has been identified as an important determinant of language acquisition in the form of preliteracy skills (Barnett, 1995; Barnett, Frede, Mobasher, & Mohr 1987).

What can be done to increase the possibility that young children receive adequate preparation in their day-care or preschool setting? Schools may work in a number of ways with preschool providers; three major efforts to increase the collaboration between school districts and preschool providers are described here. First, school districts should work collegially with preschool providers so that there is a clear understanding of (1) what schools expect from entering kindergarteners, and (2) what educational experiences students receive in their preschool settings. Schools also need to know what providers value and why their programs include various activities and experiences. Gathering this information can be accomplished in several ways: (1) Schools can share the list of standards or competencies for entering kindergarten; (2) preschool providers can also share their curriculum; (3) teachers from the two sites can visit each others' classrooms to get a better understanding of students' experiences; and (4) meetings between the two groups of teachers can bridge the gap that often occurs and eliminate, or at least reduce, the "blame" game.

Second, and as important, preschool providers who educate students for a district should be included in the various professional development programs that are available. When school districts convene a professional development meeting in which the speaker is addressing an issue important for the education of young children, invitations can be extended to the preschool providers. It may not be possible for all preschool teachers to attend, but perhaps arrangements can be made so that there is some sharing of information.

Third, when opportunities for working together arise, seize them! At the present time, the interest in early learning is not only creating such opportunities, it is *demanding* them. Possible proposals for funding can be investigated and written, and community collaboration for such endeavors can be cultivated.

Reading specialists can assume an important role in promoting each of these three steps. Indeed, reading specialists are often the ones who need to "create" opportunities for working together. They can certainly foster interaction between kindergarten and preschool teachers, especially in the discussion about literacy instruction. They may also be able to provide professional development for the preschool teachers.

## Libraries

Reading specialists, of course, need to be involved with the librarians responsible for the school library, ensuring that there are a variety of books that promote learning in the school. Equally important, the school librarian must develop experiences for students that create an excitement and enthusiasm for reading. The community library is also a resource for the school. Most community libraries assign a staff member to interact with personnel from schools who are eager to participate in school–library collaborations. The reading specialist who takes the time to work with the community librarian is likely to find new ways to enhance student motivation to read. Some of the ways that schools and libraries can work together include the following:

• Librarians can come to school to read books to children and to solicit membership in the community library. After reading a book, it can be left in the classroom for follow-up work by the teacher.

• Students can visit the community library on a field trip; here the librarian leads the students through the various sections of the library, explaining the types of resources offered by each.

• The school and library personnel can work together to develop a summer program for students. This program can be promoted in the school and recognition given at the school in the fall for those students who complete the program. Research findings indicate that there is a "summer slide" for children of poverty; that is, children from higher socioeconomic groups do not experience the summer learning loss that characterizes those in lower socioeconomic groups (Alexander, Entwisle, & Olson, 2001). Allington and McGill Frazen (1989) indicated that it is important for children to have many opportunities to read during the summer. I would encourage reading specialists to work with the community library to create programs that benefit both successful and struggling readers.

• The reading specialist can inform the librarian about special school initiatives, for example, specific reading programs or efforts that require specific books. Often, the librarian will then make certain that those books are included in the library's collections.

Recently, a library and school district in an urban setting collaborated to develop a special library program designed to promote reading in schools where there were large numbers of struggling readers. This program, funded by a local foundation, was designed to (1) stimulate motivation by introducing multicultural books, and (2) enhance reading achievement by introducing and discussing various vocabulary words from those texts. Personnel from the library went to the third-grade classrooms twice a month to read and discuss a multicultural book with the children, and then left the book in the classroom. Evaluation of that program indicated that students really enjoyed listening to the book and that they often selected and read the book on their own. Teachers felt the program enhanced students' reading interest, and they (the teachers) enjoyed learning about new trade books they could then use in their classroom work.

## Community-Based Programs

In many communities, especially those in poverty areas, programs operated by churches or community agencies are available. These programs provide a safe place for children whose parents may be working, and, as important, they reinforce school lessons by helping students with homework or providing tutoring and academic support. Recent legislation has deemed faith-based organizations eligible to apply for approval to provide supplemental educational services to low-income students attending underachieving schools. Such services can provide help before or after school, on weekends or during the summer, in both reading and math.

These organizations, whether faith- or community-based, can support or extend the work of the school. In order to help them achieve their goals in ways that facilitate the work of the school, reading specialists or other school personnel need to become involved in two major ways. First, schools need to communicate with agencies offering these services so that there is an awareness of what additional support students are receiving. Second, schools can increase the effectiveness of these community programs by providing training or guidance in terms of what strategies or instructional support would be most congruent with classroom instruction. For example, if students in a school are working with a specific program or curriculum, the school might suggest that the community-based program use the supplemental books that are aligned with that program. A check sheet might be devised for classroom teachers, so that they can easily communicate the needs of specific students (e.g., "J needs to practice his new sight words. I'm including them in this packet.")

## Universities and Colleges

Many schools are close enough to universities to be able to partner with them on various projects that bring preservice teachers, volunteers, or faculty into their schools. Faculty involved with preservice education programs look for ways to form partnerships with schools in which there is quality instruction based on best practice and with mentors who are excellent role models. Many are eager to cooperate in many different ways: teaching classes on site and recruiting classroom teachers willing to participate; providing up-to-date resources and information to schools; and holding meetings in which there is in-depth discussion about what preservice students are learning and its congruence with the instruction occurring in the classrooms.

Many faculty at universities and colleges also appreciate opportunities to participate in professional development efforts of schools, or they are interested in conducting research that will contribute to the understanding of how students learn to read. Although such partnerships need to be entered into thoughtfully, so that there is a clear understanding of the benefits for each partner, these ventures can be the catalyst for much growth for both. In a previous chapter, I described the LEADERS project in which we worked with several school districts on a professional development initiative. The outcome of the project included not only changes in classroom teacher practices and student achievement; in addition, university faculty learned a great deal about what works in schools, what is difficult to implement, and the problems that must be addressed in efforts to improve the quality of literacy instruction.

Volunteers, of course, can come from many different sources: senior citizens, retired teachers, parents, as well as college students. They can also come from the business sector. Because of the work–study portion of the America Reads Challenge Act of 1997, which provided funding for college students who were eligible for work–study to become volunteer tutors in the schools, many colleges and universities sent their students into schools or community agencies to tutor struggling readers. Much has been written about the results of the America Reads efforts (Fitzgerald, 2001; Morrow & Woo, 2001), and various manuals and procedures for implementing programs have been developed (Bader, 1998; Johnson, Juel, & Invernizzi, 1995). Bean, Turner, and Belski (2003) discuss lessons learned from implementing such a program, identifying issues that need to be addressed by university and school or community-based personnel.

The next section discusses guidelines for working with volunteer tutors and paraprofessionals.

## Volunteers and Paraprofessionals in the Schools

Volunteer efforts in schools are becoming more and more common, as is the use of paraprofessionals. In fact, given the increased number of paraprofessionals in schools to supplement the work of teachers, the newly revised International Reading Association standards (2003) indicate that reading specialists need to work effectively with paraprofessionals by helping them to plan lessons, observing them with students, providing feedback about their performance, providing staff development training, and providing emotional and academic support. The standards also include a list of competencies for paraprofessionals.

In the past, parents volunteered to come into schools to help teachers. Often they did clerical work, duplicating worksheets, correcting papers, or they assisted in cafeteria or playground duty. Currently, there is much more emphasis on using volunteers or paraprofessionals to assist with instruction, providing opportunities for students to practice reading orally, reviewing sight words, and helping with student writing. Such volunteer programs can be informal, with parents or tutors following the lead or suggestions of teachers to whom they have been assigned, or much more formal, with volunteers or paraprofessionals serving as tutors for children experiencing difficulties. On pages 33–37, Lucy Klocksin discusses her efforts to train parent volunteers to work with primary students. Lapp, Fisher, Flood, and Frey (2003) described what they call "ride along" tutoring, in which reading specialists train, monitor, and support aides who provide one-to-one instruction to struggling readers.

Often the reading specialist is responsible for recruiting, training, and directing the work of paraprofessionals and volunteers in the school. One reading specialist in a local school was responsible for directing the work of more than 17 tutors who worked with primary children in her building. She had a massive job of coordinating schedules, training these tutors, and then monitoring their work and the progress of students. The following guidelines may be helpful to those interested in initiating such programs in their schools.

1. *Provide adequate training for volunteers or paraprofessionals.* Wasik (1998) reported that in successful tutoring programs, reading specialists (a) trained and provided feedback to volunteer tutors, and (b) wrote and supervised lessons. In other words, tutoring programs may not be successful if careful supervision of tutors is lacking. Indeed, an unsupervised program can result in wasted time and money. On the other hand, Baker, Gersten, and Keating (2000) described a volunteer tutoring program in which community volunteers were given brief training and a broad framework from which to plan. Students in the experimental group exhibited greater growth on several dimensions of reading, compared to students in the comparison group who received no tutoring. This study indicated that even minimally trained tutors can facilitate progress in struggling readers. The Baker study, and a later one by Fitzgerald (2002), indicated that there is much we do not know about tutoring by volunteers. The caring relationship that is built between the volunteer and the child may be a key element in motivating the child to do better in school. The gains, of course, may have been greater with additional training of volunteers. However, in instances

where fiscal or logistical restrictions limit the amount of training or supervision, leaders can still develop a tutoring program that can have a positive effect on students and their reading performance.

Tutoring programs currently available, such as Reading One-to-One (Farkas, Warrren, & Johnson, 1999), provide specific directions and materials for tutors so that they understand what they need to do to work successfully with children. In our work with America Reads tutors, we found that they needed assistance in how to motivate and keep children interested in learning, given their lack of experience in working with children. A successful program may require a literacy coordinator who is responsible for the training, monitoring, and evaluation of that program.

2. *Help tutors understand the school culture, school procedures, and regulations.* Many volunteer tutors have little understanding or experience with schools, other than the ones they attended, often many years ago! Volunteers need to be given specific information about school rules and regulations, appropriate dress, and behavior. They need assistance in understanding how to communicate with the classroom teacher and the rules to be followed if the child is not behaving (i.e., what are the specific disciplinary procedures followed by the school or the classroom teacher?) The time spent on these topics is appreciated by tutors and creates a better atmosphere for cooperation and collaboration between school personnel and tutors.

3. *Seek input from, and provide feedback to, classroom teachers.* Classroom teachers can provide useful information about children and their reading needs. They can also provide information as to whether there are changes in the child's performance as the tutoring progresses. At the same time, the classroom teacher should be informed about the tutoring, its emphasis, and given feedback as to how the child is performing in the tutoring session. Teachers may be more receptive to the tutoring, which may pull students from classroom instruction, if they have input into the tutoring plan. Classroom teachers should have occasions to meet and talk with tutors. Often they can provide ideas to tutors about working with specific children.

4. *Monitor and evaluate the program.* The reading specialist responsible for the tutoring program should have a means of monitoring the work of each tutor and determining whether a child is making progress. If there is little or no progress, changes need to be made. The reading specialist should have a system for evaluating the overall program. If the program is successful, great! But if the program is

showing little in the way of results, there must be discussion about how it can be improved.

One of the criticisms of tutoring programs is that they are not aligned with the classroom instruction. This is a legitimate concern that should be addressed by those responsible for the tutoring program. In evaluating the program, the reading specialist can develop and send questionnaires to teachers and parents to determine program effects. Student outcomes can also be investigated, using formal or informal assessment measures.

## WORKING WITH FAMILIES

Given the requirements in Title 1 regulations, many reading specialists have played a special role in promoting family involvement. They have had to keep parents apprised of the supplemental instruction received by students who have reading difficulties. They must also communicate with parents in various ways and on a regular basis so that parents gain an understanding of what they can do to enhance the reading performance of their children. Specialists may also need to develop comprehensive family literacy programs, in which parents receive literacy instruction.

The awareness of the importance of family involvement has generated policies and procedures at all levels of government—federal, state, local—and has affected school programs and practices. The following sections discuss various ways in which reading specialists can work with parents and families to ensure greater literacy performance for children. First, several important guidelines are described.

1. *School personnel must have an understanding of the families whose children they serve.* In today's schools, many teachers do not live in the communities they serve, and for that reason may lack an indepth understanding of the culture and experiences of their students. Teachers may believe that children are not learning because of their backgrounds or the lack of support from home. And although the educational task may be more difficult when children do not arrive at the school door with expected literacy experiences or skills, teachers with an understanding and appreciation of the talents and experiences that children *do* bring can be more effective in working with them. Some schools have asked

teachers to conduct home visits; others schedule parent conferences in neighborhood agencies that are close to children's homes (especially necessary when children are bussed to schools a far distance from their homes). The reading specialist can serve as a catalyst for helping teachers gain knowledge and understanding of students, their background, and their culture.

2. *School personnel must help parents understand their academic and behavioral goals and expectations for children.* Although schools continue to communicate through written materials, others have begun to develop telephone networks or computer hotlines where parents can find information online.

3. *School personnel should create an environment that welcomes parents into the schools.* Too many parents, especially those who themselves were not successful in school, are not comfortable going into classrooms. As mentioned above, parents may serve as volunteers and paraprofessionals in providing direct service to students. These parents then know a great deal about the schools! Parents can also assist by making presentations to classes about their professions, serving as reader-of-the-day or week, and acting as supervisors on field trips. In one school, the coordinator of a special reading project developed a program in which parents were responsible for reading a book and then presenting a craft or art activity to the children. The coordinator helped parents select the book and the activity, and the teacher assisted with the lesson and any management problems. Parents were delighted with the teaching experience and the added bonus of seeing their child in the classroom context. Children were excited that their mom or dad was going to teach (and other children often acknowledged the fact that "Billy's mom is teaching today!"). At a celebration breakfast these parents talked about their increased appreciation for the teaching profession—and the teachers of their children! (Teaching is not as easy as they thought.)

In another school, the individual responsible for federal programs held four evening meetings a year, to which students brought their families. These meetings were based on a theme; for example, teachers had read *Where the Wild Things Are* (1988) by Maurice Sendak and then each class constructed a large monster drawing to be hung in the school gym. Children and parents arrived at the gym in the early evening to construct masks, to listen to another reading of the book, and to sample light refreshments. The local book store sent a "monster" to walk around the gym and decide which of the classes' monsters was the very best. Attendance at these events ranged from 100–250 participants and included parents, children and their siblings, grandparents, and interested relatives!

Results of a survey on family and school partnerships (National Center for Educational Statistics, 1996) indicated that parents are more likely to attend meetings if there is some possibility of interacting with their child's teachers. It is necessary to know the community and families and to provide what works.

4. *Parent involvement should extend through the grades.* It is true that parent involvement declines with each grade level, showing the most dramatic decrease at the point of transition into the middle grades (Billig, 2002). Nevertheless opportunities to build parent involvement in the middle grades are available. Billig suggests that too often the communication during middle and high school years tends to be one-way—from the school to the family—and recommends the following five guidelines for schools seeking to form strong partnerships with parents (2002, pp. 43–45):

    a. Use the challenges of the middle school years to build parent involvement programs. Students will now face more demanding academics and be asked to assume more responsibility.

    b. Build on the need and value that middle schoolers place on strong relationships.

    c. Encourage parent and student participation in decision making. Parents and students can be involved in curriculum decisions, e.g., selection of textbooks.

    d. Train school faculty to work well with parents, how to communicate, how to report student progress, work with volunteers, and become involved with community partnerships.

    e. Keep families informed about what students are learning.

## PRACTICAL IDEAS FOR INCREASING PARENT INVOLVEMENT IN THE SCHOOLS

This section describes ideas for increasing parent involvement in the schools and resources that may be helpful.

1. *Create a parent involvement program that is an integral part of the school reading program.* Too often, parent involvement efforts are idio-

syncratic, that is, they differ from teacher to teacher. Effective programs, however, require procedures for reflecting on what is being done and a systematic effort to involve parents in their children's educational process. This effort includes involving parents in the decision making about the plan itself (what do parents need and want?); and securing a long-term commitment to the plan on the part of teachers and parents alike. Sometimes it is necessary to educate teachers about how to work effectively with families; often it means rethinking what parent involvement means in a specific school or community. In other words, teachers, administrators, and reading specialists should decide as a group what means will be used to communicate with and inform parents. Such a plan may include ideas for formal events such as parent workshops or conferences. It may also include ideas for communicating with parents on a regular basis about the accomplishments of their children. The plan may also indicate who is responsible for the various activities (e.g., the reading specialist will plan a meeting that provides suggestions for parents on how they can help their children become better readers, all teachers will send home a "positive" note to parents at least once a semester).

2. *Take every opportunity to communicate with parents, and use many different approaches to communication.* Effective teachers have always reinforced the positive. They send home notes telling parents what their child has done well, reinforced a child's behavior with stickers or a certificate, or even called parents to tell them how "Johnny made my day." In today's world, we need to take advantage of the technology available to communicate with parents. One kindergarten teacher creates a photograph album of her class, with digital pictures and a caption dictated by the child. At the end of the year, this teacher holds a kindergarten graduation at which she shows these photos to the attending parents. Each parent also receives a copy of the album. Student success is celebrated! This teacher has no difficulty with parent attendance. She also communicates on a weekly basis with parents, sending a letter that tells them what students have learned that week and how parents can reinforce the learning. Other teachers communicate via e-mail messages; some have cell phones, and parents are told they can call a designated number at a specific time to raise questions or address concerns.

In addition to these individual efforts that teachers make, there should be a systematic plan for communicating with parents, K–12. Newsletters and bulletins are useful, especially if they include many practical ideas for parents. Some schools send home a calendar over the summer that suggests a literacy activity that children can do each day or week.

Reading specialists can develop their own material to send home to parents, or they can select from material that is available. Figure 9.1 is a handout for parents with tips for reading to their child that was distributed by the Keystone State Reading Association, Committee on Parents and Children. Figure 9.2 is a list of references for adults of what books are available for children of all ages.

In one community, foundations provided support to place large billboards, displaying a picture of a mother reading to her young child, near major highways. The goal was to generate awareness of the importance of reading and to motivate families to read to their children.

Reading specialists can develop and hold workshops and meetings that increase parents' understanding of how important they are to the literacy learning of their children. Ideas about how to help children develop a love of reading and providing an environment that encourages reading can be shared. Parents can be given specific ideas about how to read effectively to their children and how to listen to their children read to them. Two important resources that provide specific ideas include *Families at School: A Guide for Educators* (Thomas, Fazio, & Stiefelmeyer, 1999a) and *Families at School: A Handbook for Parents* (Thomas, Fazio, & Stiefelmeyer, 1999b).

3. *Provide training that improves teachers' ability to talk or conference with parents.* Some guidelines that may be helpful include the following:

- Be prepared. Have examples of student work easily at hand so that parents can be shown what their child can and cannot do. As noted, it is important to talk about what the child *can* do and to emphasize the positive.
- Try to refrain from using school talk or jargon. Parents may not be familiar with such terms as "phonemic" or "phonological awareness," "fluency," or concepts about print. It is best to *show* parents what is challenging their child.
- Try to establish a friendly but professional atmosphere in the conference. It is preferable for the reading specialist to avoid sitting behind his or her desk; a table is more welcoming and still provides the surface area for various materials and work samples.
- Talk only about the child and what he or she can do. Do not compare the child with others.

- Read aloud to your child every day, even an older child. Reading aloud provides a good model, expands vocabulary, stimulates curiosity and imagination, lengthens attention span, and motivates the child to want to read better books independently. Most important of all, it helps to develop a lifetime reader! Be sure to "ham it up" when reading aloud.
- Share reading with your child by alternate reading. You read a page and then your child reads a page. Or you read a paragraph and your child reads a paragraph.
- Be aware that reading level and listening level are different.
  −Read easy books with your child.
  −Read more advanced books to your child to instill motivation and a love of books.
- For an older child, read aloud the first few chapters of a book to get him or her started. This is where the characters are introduced, the plot is set up, and the setting is described. You'll be offering a jump start!
- Discuss the book you're reading together:
  −Predict what the book will be about before reading it.
  −Talk about the pictures.
  −Periodically stop and predict what will happen next.
  −Consider what else could have happened.
  −Relate the story to your own experiences.
  −Stop to explain things you think your child does not know.
  −Talk about the author and illustrator.
- Carry books with you wherever you go; read to your child while waiting for appointments, for example.
- Tape-record favorite books so your young child can listen to them over and over, even in the car.
- Choose repetitive, rhythmic books for younger readers, and look for interesting illustrations that help to tell the story.
- Take time each day for everyone in the family to read silently; show you value reading by allowing your child to see you read.
- Encourage your child to keep a journal by recording the day's happenings, his or her feelings, etc.
- Provide pencils, pens, crayons, markers, paper, and other materials for your child to use to express feelings and thoughts about what is read.
- Give your child his or her own library card for the public library; visit the library often.
- Encourage your child to read easy books to improve fluency.
- Subscribe to children's magazines.
- Write notes to your child and tuck them into a lunch box or pocket.
- Enjoy reading with your child.

**FIGURE 9.1.** Tips for reading with your child (from Keystone State Reading Association).

Cullinan, B., & Bagert, B. *Helping Your Child Learn to Read*. Available for free through *How to Help Your Child Learn to Read*, Dept. 617Z, Consumer Information Center, Pueblo, CO 81009.

Cullinan, B. E. (2000). *Read to Me: Raising Kids Who Love to Read*. New York: Scholastic.

Kimmel, M. M., & Segel, E. (1988). *For Reading Out Loud!: A Guide to Sharing Books with Children*. New York: Delacorte Press.

Larrick, N. (1982). *A Parent's Guide to Children's Reading* (5th ed.). Philadelphia: Westminster.

Lipson, E. R. (2000). *The New York Times Parent's Guide to the Best Books for Children* (3rd ed.). New York: Three Rivers Press.

Trelease, J. (Ed.). (1992). *Hey! Listen to This: Stories to Read Aloud!* New York: Viking.

Trelease, J. (1989). *The New Read-Aloud Handbook* (2nd rev. ed.). New York: Penguin.

**FIGURE 9.2.** Resource list of children's books for adults.

---

- Be a good listener. Reading specialists learn so much more if they solicit information from parents, who, after all, may be able to provide additional understanding of how to work with their child. No matter how divergent their point of view, it will enhance the reading specialist's grasp of the Big Picture.

It is a rare parent who does not want his or her child to be successful. It is our responsibility to solicit their participation in their children's learning process.

## SUMMARY

This chapter discussed the rationale for building partnerships with communities and families and described various ways in which reading specialists can work to build relationships with community agencies, including preschool providers, universities, libraries, those who offer supplemental programs to students, and volunteers. In addition, the importance of parents' involvement, and ways of enhancing that involvement, in their children's education were discussed.

## Reflections

1. Why would some parents feel uncomfortable about meeting with a teacher? How could this discomfort be alleviated?
2. What activities and programs does your local library offer that enhance reading performance of students in the school? How could your school partner with the local library?

## Activities

1. Develop a friendly newsletter for parents that provides them with ideas about how they can work effectively with their children. The newsletter can be one for parents of students in a specific age group (i.e., preschool, primary, intermediate, middle school, or secondary).
2. Using the guidelines in this chapter, practice holding a conference with a parent, using one of the scenarios described below. Role-play in threes— one person is the family member, the other is the teacher or reading specialist, and the third is the observer who provides feedback about the conference.

> *Scenario 1: Sally.* Sally's mom is concerned about her daughter's performance in school. She does not understand why Sally is receiving help from the reading specialist. Sally is a fourth grader at an urban elementary school. She is coming to the reading specialist because she is having difficulty in her social studies and science classes. She received all A's in reading and spelling in grades 1, 2, and 3, but this year she seems to be having trouble with her content subjects. She complains to her mom that she can read the words but she does not know what they mean, and that when she gets to the end of a passage or chapter, she cannot remember anything she has read.
>
> Sally, an only child, has always lived with her mother and grandmother, who both work. Finances are limited, and Sally has not had many opportunities that might enrich her literacy background. Although her caretakers have tried to take her to the museum and to the local zoo, etc., time is limited (given their work schedules). There are few books in the home, and although the mother indicates that she would love to read to Sally, she is tired at the end of the day, and somehow there never seems to be time. Sally has good health; she wears

glasses (although she forgets them much of the time). She also loves school and her teachers (except for the social studies teacher—who keeps asking her difficult questions). She also loves books—especially storybooks. She hates her content subjects, though, because "everything is just too hard" (or so she tells her mom). She has always received praise from her reading teachers for her excellent reading—she loves to read orally—and with expression. She cannot understand why she is unable to comprehend her new books in fourth grade.

*Scenario 2: Henry.* Henry's parents have come for a consultation about Henry's poor grades. They are eager to help him. Henry is a ninth-grade student at a suburban high school. He is getting D's and F's in courses such as American literature and history. He does fairly well in algebra and biology. Henry moved to this high school from a small rural school this past year. He had always been an average student in school. He knows that he is a slow reader and that he often has difficulty figuring out the words. Once he knows the words, he realizes that he does know the meaning. He does not read much, but when he does read, he chooses material about dog care (he has a Lab that he trains) or magazines dealing with the outdoors. He cannot remember reading a book that was not required reading. He likes classes where he does not have to read much—and he hates to write. (His handwriting is slow and laborious.) He does love working on the computer, though, and his parents have agreed to get one (he is really excited about that). Math is his favorite area, and he likes science too (especially biology).

Henry is the oldest boy of four children (he has an older sister and two younger twin brothers). All of his siblings are excellent readers, and Henry realizes that he is the one who has the most difficulty in school. His parents try to help him with his schoolwork, but he does not like to bother them because they have lots of things to do with his younger brothers. The family is very supportive of all the children. Henry has decided to go out for the track team, and he knows that his family will attend all of the games.

Henry has good vision and hearing. He had one serious illness in second grade, when he missed a great deal of school and was tutored at home for almost 3 months. Since that time, he has not had any difficulty with his health. He has always had difficulty with reading, especially after his return to school in second grade.

# 10

## *Writing Proposals*

The Superintendent is excited about the potential of obtaining additional funds from the state to develop a summer school for struggling readers. The Title 1 proposal is due soon, and the reading specialist has the responsibility for writing it.

There is an opportunity to obtain funds from a local foundation to upgrade computers in the school, if a proposal is submitted that demonstrates how the use of such computers will be integrated into classroom instruction.

Teachers can obtain mini-grants by writing a proposal for a special classroom project.

In today's world, there are many opportunities for obtaining additional funds to support schools' efforts to provide instruction to its students. At times, reading specialists in the schools may be required to write proposals to obtain Title 1 funds, special state funding, or foundation grants. Reading specialists may also take the initiative to write the proposals because they see the possibility of improving the reading program with additional support. There are many different types of proposals, and requirements differ. For example, research proposals often require lengthy submissions, with a review of literature and research that supports the plan. On the other hand, some proposals for obtaining materials or developing a special program may be quite short, requiring only the rationale, the plan for use or implementation, and a budget. All proposals have some characteristics in common, however. This chapter presents general guidelines for writing a proposal, the various parts of a proposal, and suggestions for developing each part.

## GENERAL GUIDELINES FOR PROPOSAL WRITING

1. *Develop a great idea!* No matter how well written or how elaborate a proposal is, without a great idea, it will not be an effective outreach tool for obtaining funding. Reviewers look for an idea that is creative or well developed or one that addresses an important topic. For example, if there is concern about the fact that primary students are regressing in their reading performance over the summer, coming up with a creative idea for motivating children and families to read over the summer may be the key to obtaining funds from a local foundation.

Just as authors stress the importance of writing about a topic known well to the writer, so too do great ideas for grants come from immersion in the work that needs the funding. The content or ideas in a proposal should be based on reading specialists' expertise, interests, and knowledge of the field (i.e., what has been done and what has worked). Often these ideas come from discussions with colleagues, attendance at a conference, or from reading an article in a professional journal.

2. *Locate a good match.* A reading specialist seeking funds to undertake a specific project must try to locate funders whose priorities match the proposed activities or initiative. The reading specialist would not, for example, send a proposal for a professional development project to a funding agency that indicates they are seeking proposals for summer programs for children. Several useful resources are available for those who wish to write proposals to seek additional funds to support their efforts:

*http://www.schoolgrants.org*
*Grants for K–12*, Quinlan Publishing Group.
Orlich, D. C. (1996). *Designing Successful Grant Proposals*. Alexan-

dria, VA: Association for Supervision and Curriculum Development.

3. *Proposal should be well written.* This is, of course, easy to say but much more difficult to do. Funders do not look favorably on proposals that have grammatical errors or are difficult to read (e.g., they are difficult to follow or lack meaningful transitions between parts). The following tips should be helpful in thinking about this guideline:

- Use the terminology and organization suggested in the proposal application. If the application calls for a discussion of objectives followed by plan of implementation, use those terms to identify those two sections of the proposal. If the application requires two specific types of evaluation (e.g., formative and summative), write the proposal to address those two dimensions. This is a place where creativity may count against the writer!
- Follow the rules. The submission should not have more than the required number of pages, it should arrive on or before the designated closing date, it should display the appropriate font size, and so on. The writer also needs to address the priorities mentioned in the proposal. If the funding is offered for students who have been identified as coming from high poverty areas, receiving a proposal in which the population of students does not qualify as such will immediately disqualify it from consideration by the funding agency.

4. *Talk to funders.* It is very appropriate to call and ask questions of those who want to fund proposals. After all, they have put out a call, wanting to give funds to worthy recipients. Generally, they are more than willing to answer questions about the proposal before the closing date. Grant writers should feel free to call or e-mail the funder to discuss their ideas or to raise questions about the proposal application itself. If there is a preproposal session, held for potential writers, it would be beneficial to attend those sessions. In one instance, I was able to collaborate with two other educators in writing a staff development proposal, since we had all attended the preproposal session and had an opportunity to sit and talk about our ideas.

5. *Solicit feedback.* Writing is a lonely task, and, too often, writers think that what they have written is very clear! Soliciting feedback from a colleague is a wonderful way to determine whether the content makes

sense, if there is enough detail, and if any technical problems with the writing are apparent. The goal is to obtain constructive feedback based on a thoughtful, critical evaluation.

   6. *Use effective formatting.* Although a great idea is very important, even it can lose its luster in a poorly formatted presentation. A well-formatted proposal containing a great idea catches the eye and the mind of reviewers. Providing a table of contents and using section headings that guide the reader are important techniques to use. Likewise, use bold, italic, or underline fonts to highlight the important ideas. If possible, use graphics to amplify points made in the narrative text.

   7. *Become familiar with the review criteria.* Proposal guidelines often include the criteria for proposal review (e.g., indicating the number of points designated for each section). A smart proposal writer makes certain that each criterion is addressed and emphasizes the sections that are worth a significant number of points.

## ELEMENTS OF A PROPOSAL

Most proposals require each of the elements or parts discussed below. When preparing to write a proposal, it is helpful to read all of the proposal guidelines, and then, after writing various sections, reread them as a means of determining whether each of the elements has been clearly addressed. At the end of the chapter is a short proposal (Figure 10.1) written by a graduate student for a course assignment. It illustrates many of the elements discussed below, although differences exist because the writer followed the guidelines of the funding agency.

### Goals and Objectives

Although some of the other elements may not be required in a specific proposal application, all proposals require statements of goals or objectives for the potential project or program. In some proposals, only broad goals are required (e.g., increase teachers' use of computer technology in teaching reading). In other applications, however, the writer must write objectives that indicate specifically what is going to change and by how much and when:

> By the end of 5 years, we will improve the average comprehension performance of Title 1 students from 30 Normal Curve Equivalents to 50.

## Review of Literature

Not all proposals call for a review of the literature; the funding source, the amount of funding offered, and the type of proposal (i.e., research) are the common determinants of this component. When there is a requirement for such a review, the key is to identify the relevant and current literature that (1) supports the need for the project being described, and (2) summarizes what is known to date about the proposed issue or project. For example, if a reading specialist wants to develop a project for working with preschool providers, a review of literature about the importance of early learning for young students and its impact on later reading achievement would be beneficial. Such literature should include information about the need for additional knowledge in this area. The proposal in Figure 10.1 contains no literature review. However, the writer does use research to introduce her project and highlight its importance, given research evidence about the need for exposing young children to informational text.

## Project Activities or Methods

In some proposal applications, this section is referred to as the design of the project. It is here that the writer explains what he or she plans to do. The activities or design must relate to the identified objectives or goals, and there must be clear evidence that the plan will enable the writer to meet them. The writer must be certain that readers know exactly what will be done, when, and how. Examples are critical—let the readers know, by example, what will occur. Described below is an example of part of a methods sections:

> We plan to work with preschool providers in two ways. First, we will invite them to visit our kindergartens and then participate in a 2-hour discussion with the kindergarten teachers. Second, kindergarten teachers will visit the preschool programs and, again, participate in a 2-hour discussion. Our expectation is that participants will have opportunities to address issues such as the following: What are the literacy expectations and standards in kindergarten and in what ways can preschool teachers prepare students for their kindergarten experience? What experiences and activities are currently occurring in preschool programs, and how do they address the literacy needs of students?

Creating a time line for various activities is helpful not only to readers but to the writer as a means of determining exactly how the entire project or activity will be implemented. Likewise, graphics or visuals can aid readers in understanding the plan of operation.

## Personnel

Funders want to know who will work on the project and what skills and experiences they have that will enable them to accomplish the planned work. So, for example, if the reading specialist writing the proposal cited above has taught in a preschool or has already implemented such a program in another district, this experience should be described. Providing specifics about qualifications helps to assure funders that the expertise needed to undertake the project is available. Likewise, the application may call for an iteration of the resources or capabilities of the organization or institution with which the writer is affiliated. What computer resources are available to assist in data analysis? Does the institution have a testing department that can assess the success of the project? Are there other personnel who might be helpful with the project (e.g., a supportive director of curriculum, etc.)?

## Evaluation

Almost all proposals call for some form of evaluation that indicates to what extent the writer has accomplished his or her goals. Evaluation plans run the gamut of simple to complex. The two types of evaluation that may be required—formative and summative—are described below.

### Formative

Formative evaluation requires ongoing documentation of what occurs. This type of evaluation is often used to make midproject corrections or adjustments; in other words, to learn from what has transpired. In the preschool proposal example described above, formative evaluation might include documentation logs of various meetings (i.e., when they occurred and who attended) and evaluation forms completed by attendees.

### Summative

The summative evaluation provides the results of the project, in this case, the effects of the preschool–kindergarten project on participants (e.g., students, teachers, parents). The evaluation may also call for "deliverables," a manual or listing of activities developed as a result of the project.

Often, with summative evaluation, we think of effects as "changes" that have occurred. For example, a writer might propose the possibility of specific changes in teacher classroom practices. Likewise, various pre- and posttests can be administered to students to determine whether there are differences in reading performance, or attitudes toward reading, after the implementation of the project. The writer of the proposal in Figure 10.1 includes both summative and formative evaluation. In addition to documenting ongoing efforts, the writer administers a final questionnaire to teachers and parents and analyzes results of reading tests.

## Budget

All proposals naturally require a budget (since the writer is applying for funds to do something), which can be a simple or complex matter, as is the case with evaluations. For example, a budget submission may be as simple as requesting $200 to purchase books to conduct literature circles, or as the proposal in Figure 10.1 somewhat more complex, in that the writer had to identify costs for staff development in addition to hiring substitute teachers to cover classrooms while teachers attended meetings. Large proposals may require budgets that include costs for personnel, supplies, materials, travel, and so on. In some instances, the writer must include indirect or overhead costs: That is, the amount the institution will charge for housing the grant. This item covers such necessities as lighting, office space, and computer accessibility. Generally, in a school context, the school district or institution has a specific amount identified. Sometimes the funding agency supplies a ceiling amount or indicates that they do not pay overhead costs at all. Often this is the case with foundations.

## Dissemination Plan

Some proposals require that writers discuss how they will share the information they learn with others. Writers might indicate that they will present at conferences, write papers, or produce a deliverable that will be distributed to various institutions and educators.

## Continuation Plans

Although not invariably a required part of a proposal application, many funding agencies (especially foundations) ask for continuation plans because they are interested in the sustainability of various projects. Can they be assured that if they provide monies for a special project, such as a summer program, that the institution will then find a way to continue such an effort? Often, funders are discouraged that various projects are disbanded as soon as the funding is gone.

## Abstract

The all-important abstract, which is the beginning of the proposal submission, is best written after the writing is complete. Only now is the writer ready to summarize, in a few lucid paragraphs, exactly what he or she is planning to do. The abstract must catch the reader's eye (the value of a first impression) and identify the goals and activities of the proposed plan succinctly and clearly. It may also include an overview of the evaluation approaches.

## SOURCES FOR FUNDING

Many different sources of funding can be investigated to determine whether various grant possibilities exist. Generally, the education department in the state posts announcements about various state or federal funding possibilities on its website. Newsletters and websites of various professional organizations are also excellent sources for obtaining information about support (e.g., International Reading Association, Association for Supervision and Curriculum Development, National Council of Teachers of English). Local and national foundations often have calls for proposals on websites; foundation directories that describe goals and purposes of these philanthropic organizations are also available.

One of the best ways to seek funding is to work collaboratively with another institution in the area, such as a local university, library, or community agency. Funding agencies look favorably upon such collaborative efforts because the unique contributions that can be made by each partner strengthen a proposal. For example, a university can assist in the evaluation of a project designed by a school district. Or the school district and library can work together to design a summer reading program for struggling readers.

## REJECTION

A chapter on proposal writing should not end on a negative note. However, the reality is that not all proposals are funded. All of us who have written proposals have most likely received one or more rejection notices. Another reality is that the key to getting a project funded is to write it! Furthermore, rejection notices can be very helpful. I have learned that reviewers' comments can be used to rewrite and resubmit— either in a different funding cycle or to a different funding agency. Believe it or not, the second time around can be successful! Moreover, writing the proposal enables the writer to cultivate a relationship with the funding agency, increasing the potential for later success.

## SUMMARY

This chapter discussed reasons why the reading specialist may be involved in proposal writing. Guidelines for writing proposals and the various elements of a proposal were then described.

### Reflections

What opportunities to become involved with proposal writing are available to you in your current position?

### Activities

1. Interview someone who writes proposals to get his or her ideas about what it takes to write a successful one. Be prepared to discuss what you learned in class or with your colleagues.
2. Locate several proposals that have been submitted and critique them, using the ideas in this chapter (i.e., elements of a successful proposal).
3. Review the proposal in Figure 10.1 that follows and discuss each of its features with your colleagues or classmates.
4. Write a proposal that addresses the following mini-grant opportunity.

   A local foundation is willing to provide $500 to classroom teachers who wish to implement a creative project for their classroom that will enhance the reading performance of their students. The proposal should include the following elements: goals and objectives; plan of activities; time line; personnel; evaluation; and budget (describe the funds you will need and how they will be used).

FIGURE 10.1. An example of a brief proposal.

**READING INFORMATIONAL TEXTS IN PRIMARY CLASSROOMS**

**Mission Statement:**

We believe each person has value and the capability to achieve success. Through the commitment of a quality staff and the partnership with home and community, the mission of the Green Valley School District is to educate all students to ethically meet the challenges of a global society through positive life-role performances (Green Valley School District Strategic Plan, 2000).

**Introduction:**

According to Duke (2000), "In this Informational Age the importance of being able to read and write informational texts critically and well cannot be overstated. Informational literacy is central to success, and even survival, in schooling, the workplace and the community" (p. 213). Typically in today's classrooms, children are not given the opportunity to explore informational/nonfiction literature until the second or third-grade year. This omission leaves a lapse of 7 to 8 years during which children are not exposed to this type of literature. Upon entering high school and throughout their lives, most of what these children will be reading and writing is informational text. More often than not, adults read material such as newspapers, magazines, manuals, recipes, menus, directions, and brochures far more frequently than a book of fictional literature. For this reason, children should be given the opportunity to see and read informational literature as another genre available to them before they reach the high school age. As a representative of Madison Primary School in the Green Valley School District, I propose to create a program that supplies enhancing the classroom libraries of our primary school teachers with informational/nonfiction literature. This literature will be available for children in kindergarten through grade 3 to take home and read independently or with family members and to supplement the content area instruction provided in the classroom.

I am asking the Literacy Link Foundation to become a part of this project to introduce a new literature genre to our young children by donating funds to purchase books, magazines, and other necessary materials to be placed in every classroom library in Madison Primary School. As a sponsor, the Literacy Link Foundation will assist this district's educators in helping the students become knowledgeable and productive citizens through the introduction of and exposure to informational/nonfiction text. Through the early introduction of this type of text, our students will be better prepared to comprehend the informational literature they will be expected to read throughout their adult lives.

**Goals of Project:**

The goals and purpose of this program are to

- Expose primary school children to informational/nonfiction literature in their classrooms.
- Encourage the reading of informational/nonfiction literature by primary school children.
- Support primary classroom teachers in their content area instruction.

*(continued)*

The goals of this program correlate directly with the mission of the Literacy Link Foundation by providing quality learning opportunities to children at a time in their lives when this opportunity is not usually given.

The educators responsible for achieving the success of these goals and objectives are part of a district comprised of 95 professionals with an average of 15 years teaching experience. In this group, 33% has received a master's degree, and 1% has received a doctorate degree. At Madison Primary School, 354 students are guided by 18 teachers, two reading specialists, and one principal. Each member of this teaching community feels this program would be an added benefit to those attending school in the Green Valley School District. The mission of the district is by partnering quality staff with family and community members to give each student the capability to succeed within the challenges of a global society. By exposing children to the genre of literature they will be expected to read and understand in their adult lives, this program will improve their chance of success as they develop into knowledgeable and productive citizens.

**Project Activities:**

The following activities will support each of the three goals listed above:

- All teachers at Madison Primary School will introduce and read aloud to their classes at least two informational/nonfiction books each month.
   1. The teachers will select two books to be read to their classes each month.
   2. Planning for the reading of the selected books will involve writing them in their weekly lesson plans.
   3. The principal will verify that the books to be read are included in the weekly plans.
   4. Teachers will maintain a list of books read to their classes.

- Each classroom will receive copies of informational or nonfiction literature equal to the number of students in the classroom.
   1. By September 1 of each school year, a box for donated books will be placed in the libraries of the upper elementary and junior/senior high school to be given to the primary classrooms.
   2. With book fair profits (book fair is held each year in March), each teacher will select $25 worth of informational/nonfiction literature to be placed in his or her classroom libraries (district contribution).
   3. Grant funds received will be used to purchase informational/nonfiction literature for each classroom (purchase to be completed by August 1).

- Each child will be required to read at least two informational/nonfiction books each month.
   1. Beginning the second week of school, the classroom teacher or school reading specialist will place one informational/nonfiction book in child's "Book-in-a-Bag," to be read every two weeks.
   2. A classroom chart is maintained with titles of the books read by each child.

- Each classroom teacher will offer an incentive for each child to meet the above objective.
   1. Incentives for reading two informational/nonfiction books each month will become part of the classroom behavior incentive.
   2. The classroom teacher will give stickers or awards if the objective is met each month (actual reward is at the discretion of the teacher).

(continued)

- The reading specialist will offer at least one staff development course to each grade level, to focus on using informational/nonfiction literature in the classroom.
  1. The reading specialist will gather instructional methods/materials to be used by the classroom teachers. (Topics to be discussed the following school year must be submitted to the principal or reading specialist by June 1.)
  2. The reading specialist will present the content area materials at a staff development class to be held in August or September of each year.

- All reading specialists employed at Madison Primary School will assist their assigned classroom teachers with instruction, materials, and resources needed for content area instruction.
  1. The school reading specialists will discuss available materials with their teachers (in progress).
  2. The reading specialists will provide a list of materials and resources that can be used as part of instruction (in progress).
  3. The reading specialist will model at least one whole-class lesson, emphasizing the use of informational or nonfiction literature (the total number of lessons should be decided by teacher and reading specialist).

The success of this program will rely on the following actions and processes:

- All children receiving instruction at Madison Primary School will be exposed to informational/nonfiction literature in two ways: (1) easily accessible books will be placed in the classroom library, and (2) books will be read weekly to the class by the classroom teacher.

- All children receiving instruction at Madison Primary School will be encouraged to read two informational/nonfiction books each month. The "Book-in-a-Bag" program and the monthly incentives given to those who achieve this goal will support this encouragement.

- All Madison Primary School classroom teachers will be supported by the reading staff through regular discussions, staff development courses, and the modeling of effective research-based instruction.

**Evaluation:**

The project will be evaluated as follows:
1. Teachers and parents will be asked to complete a questionnaire to determine the extent to which they valued this program and why.
2. All staff development meetings will include a written evaluation form in which teachers indicate their response to the activities.
3. Reading specialists will document which reading strategies and materials they have introduced in the classrooms.
4. Students' comprehension scores on the standardized reading test given at the end of the year will be compared to scores of the previous year.

(continued)

**Program Budget and Narrative:**

| Category | Expense | Credit |
|----------|---------|--------|
| Supplies | $6,044.46 | |
| Staff Development | 1,120.00 | |
| Transportation | 200.00 | |
| Total | $7,364.46 | |
| District Contribution | | ($450.00) |
| Grant Request Total | $6,914.46 | |

**Supplies:** Informational/nonfiction literature, as quoted by **Scholastic and Scholastic.com**Include additional bookcases, as needed, for additional literature.

**Staff Development:** Four substitute teachers to provide coverage in classrooms while teachers meet for staff development.

**Transportation:** Transportation costs to collect donated materials from both the upper elementary and high schools. Transportation costs to collect materials from Scholastic warehouse.

MARSHA TURNER
**Graduate Student**
**Reading Specialist Certification Program**
**University of Pittsburgh**

# 11

## *The Reading Specialist as Lifelong Learner*
### Meeting Challenges and Changes

Marshall McLuhan once remarked about the hazards of driving "into the future using only our rearview mirror" (*http://www.thinkexist.com/English/Author/x/Author_3619__2.htm*). The statement also applies to reading specialists who have served students in schools in many different ways throughout the years—as supervisors of reading programs, remedial teachers, resource teachers, and literacy coaches. Currently, the role of reading specialist is too diverse to define it in a narrow way. Not only is the role different but so, too, are the labels: *reading specialist, literacy coach, reading consultant, literacy consultant,* among others. Yet the underlying premise for reading specialists remains one of promoting reading achievement for all students, and especially for struggling readers (International Reading Association, 2000). Fulfilling these goals can be accomplished in a number of ways, depending upon school needs, funding for specialists, and their own experiences and strengths.

The chapters in this book address the many functions that reading specialists may need to assume not only on a daily basis, but perhaps as the year or years go by, and responsibilities and roles change. The greatest challenge for reading specialists is to be prepared for those changes that may occur. Indeed, change may be generated or initiated by specialists themselves, who see that they can affect student performance more effectively in new and different ways. This chapter focuses on the reading specialist as learner, on the premise that those who stay abreast of developments in the literacy field and in education, in general, will be able to meet the challenges and changes that are sure to occur. The chapter concludes with a section on becoming a reading specialist, providing potential reading specialists with some ideas of what to expect in reading specialist certification programs, and how they might prepare for interviews for reading specialist positions.

## PROFESSIONAL DEVELOPMENT
## FOR READING SPECIALISTS

Professional development for reading specialists, as for teachers, can occur in many different ways, from reading professional journals to formal participation in classes, workshops, or meetings of professional groups. Chapter 5 discussed professional development for teachers and reading specialists' role in leading such efforts. As they spearhead such efforts, reading specialists learn as they investigate and study topics that are to be addressed. In many schools, teachers now participate in study groups in which they discuss a specific book pertinent to educational concerns or goals. Certainly, participation in groups in which teachers and reading specialists discuss a particular book, for example, *Mosaic of Thought* (Keene & Zimmerman, 1997), generates new ideas and expands knowledge of specific topics.

Many reading specialists choose to continue their formal education by taking classes at a university or attending professional meetings. Reading specialists can also join, and become active in, one or more professional organizations; becoming a member of the network of educators involved in the organization promotes ongoing learning and sustained motivation. Reading specialists may become members of their local and state reading associations as well as the International Reading Association, whose professional journals, website, and other resources are invaluable to practicing reading specialists. Other groups that may be appropriate, depending on the grade level and responsibilities of specific reading specialists, include:

American Library Association
Association for Supervision and Curriculum Development
College Reading Association
International Society for Technology in Education
National Association for Education of Young Children
National Council of Teachers of English
National Middle School Association
National Reading Conference

In addition to attendance at various meetings and the professional development that occurs in schools, reading specialists must continue to read professional journals and books as a means of keeping current not only of what is known about reading instruction and assessment, but to understand the political and social climate in which they work. Several up-to-date references that may be helpful to reading specialists include Alvermann and Phelps (2002); Block and Pressley (2002); Farstrup and Samuels (2002); Glazer (1998); Richek, Caldwell, Jennings, and Lerner (2002); and Strickland and Morrow (2000). U.S. Government publications such as the Report of the National Reading Panel (National Institute of Child Health and Human Development, 2000) and Put Reading First (Armbruster & Osborn, 2001) are also essential reading, given their potential impact on reading instruction and assessment in schools.

The three reading specialists whose vignettes appear in this book are examples of educators who are lifelong learners. All have participated in formal education to obtain advanced degrees, all attend and present at various conferences and workshops, and all are readers who keep abreast of what is occurring in their field.

## LOCAL, STATE, AND FEDERAL GUIDELINES

Educators in today's schools face many challenging and complex political and social issues. Reading specialists must keep current on the various school-related legislative actions at local, state, and federal levels. As described in Chapter 7, the recent No Child Left Behind legislation has certainly had an impact on schools: It has influenced the assessment tools being used, has made accountability a key issue for individual teachers and for schools, and has affected curriculum and instruction, especially for reading instruction K–3. Because so many reading specialists are funded with monies from Title 1 legislation, there is certainly a need for reading specialists to be aware of the various regulations of that program.

Likewise, rules and regulations for each state influence the literacy curriculum. The emphasis on standards creates a real need for reading specialists to be aware of how to assist their colleagues in implementing an instructional program that addresses those standards. (The standards developed by states and the English/Language Arts standards formulated by the International Reading Association and National Council of Teachers of English are also important resources for reading specialists.)

As mentioned in Chapter 5, reading specialists should share information with the teachers with whom they work. In addition to the professional development opportunities described above, one helpful source that provides an update about many trends in education is the publication *Education Week*. A school subscription to that journal keeps educators aware of what is happening at the national level in relation to the field of education.

## LIFELONG LEARNING: A NECESSITY FOR READING SPECIALISTS

Given the many variables that affect the position of reading specialist and the changes that may occur from year to year within a school—some prescribed by legislation or school needs, others from recommendations by reading specialists themselves—reading specialists must remain lifelong learners. Suggestions for enacting this unwritten mandate follow.

### Set Learning Goals

Perhaps the specialist wants to involve parents more actively in school programs; perhaps the specialist wants to become more involved with teachers of content. Whatever the specific goal, the reading specialist needs to set a goal, identify activities that facilitate its achievement, and set a deadline for accomplishment. Attending one or more conferences, reading several articles or books about the selected topic, and then meeting and sharing the information with teachers (possibly forming a study group) are examples of lifelong learning activities.

## Be Prepared to Change or Modify Past or Current Behavior

One of the most difficult steps for all of us is to realize that we may have to give up what we have been doing if we are going to make changes that will make us more effective in our roles. Reading specialists who have always worked in a pullout setting may find it difficult to switch to working in the classroom. They may even grieve a little as they lose what they have always found to be a comfortable and rewarding approach to instruction. Grieving is fine, but it is important to *move on* and experience the rewards of the new and different.

## Self-Recognition

All of us appreciate the rewards and recognition that come from others—the principal who commends the work that I have done with struggling readers, the parent who tells me of the positive effect that I have had on her child. Similarly, reading specialists need to "pat themselves on the back" for what they have accomplished regarding their own learning. After finishing a professional book on assessment approaches for classroom teachers, it is time for a special dinner, a week without any professional reading (just a good mystery), or some other activity or experience that is pleasurable and rewarding.

## See Problems as Friends

There will always be demands and problems within the school setting that need the attention of the reading specialist (e.g., working with a recalcitrant teacher, improving writing scores, planning a professional development program for middle school content teachers). These demands or problems should not be seen as burdens or obstacles but as problems that generate active thinking, the opportunity for group interaction, and the possibility of new and exciting ventures in the school.

## Self-Reflection

Chapter 5 discusses the importance of teacher reflection to personal learning. Likewise, reading specialists need to take time to reflect on, and think about, what they have been doing, what they have learned, and what this learning means for future behavior. Recently, a teacher who had just completed a professional development experience expressed this thought: "It's more than learning a lot of strategies. It's thinking in a different way." In essence, her statement revealed that she was taking the time to reflect not only on her teaching methods—on what worked and what did not work—but also to consider the paradigm underlying those old methods and allow a new paradigm to form in support of the new methods. That reflection provided her with the impetus to seek new solutions to classroom problems. Taking the time for reflection means setting time aside (perhaps at the end of the day) to think about what happened and why, and the impact of that experience on future behavior.

By living as a lifelong learner, the reading specialist models for others in the school the behavior that is necessary for the school as an organization to change in order to become more effective. Leaders within a school provide the impetus for others to also become lifelong learners.

## BECOMING A READING SPECIALIST

When I ask those who enter the reading specialist certification program at my institution why they have chosen to do so, they often tell me that they have become curious about students in their classrooms who have reading difficulties and wonder how they can better help them to achieve. Some tell me that they feel unprepared to teach reading, given the few courses they received in their teacher preparation programs. Some want to work especially with struggling readers, whereas others are clear that they do not really want to leave the classroom; rather they want to become more proficient at teaching reading and meeting the needs of all students in their classrooms.

These are all good reasons for entering a reading specialist training program. Most universities have well-developed programs that meet the standards required of their state and of the International Reading Association (1998). Such programs require students to become knowledgeable about the underlying theoretical bases for literacy development and acquisition, literacy assessment and instruction, and issues related to leadership and working with others. They usually require students to participate in a practicum or clinical experience in which they demonstrate that they can fulfill the requirements of the position. Most also offer many practical experiences as an integral part of their programs, so that reading specialist candidates become proficient in working with struggling readers.

As completion of the program draws near, candidates begin to think about applying for positions as a reading specialist. They are curious about possible questions that they may be asked and how they can prepare for the interviews that generally are part of the application process. Questions that may be part of an interview are discussed in Appendix B. Candidates for a reading specialist position may wish to think about the questions and how they would answer them. Those in classes in a reading specialist certification program may role-play an interview, using some of the questions identified there.

In addition to acquiring the knowledge and understanding needed to become a reading specialist, another important attribute of any candidate for such a position is enthusiasm. School district personnel want to employ individuals who are excited and enthusiastic about becoming a reading specialist and thereby having the opportunity to make a difference for all the students in a school.

Candidates for positions may want to reread the notes that they have taken in their coursework. They may also want to read several articles in which roles of reading specialists are described. One by Bean, Swan, and Knaub (2003), in which the many roles of reading specialist in exemplary reading programs are listed, and one by Lapp, Fisher, Flood, and Frey (2003) that describes the dual role of reading specialists in an urban setting may be helpful. Rereading the vignettes of the three reading specialists found in this text may also provide candidates with a better idea of what reading specialists may be asked to do. Each of these reading specialists exhibits passion and enthusiasm for her position, regardless of the challenges or problems faced.

## SUMMARY

This chapter describes ways in which reading specialists can continue their learning and become, indeed, lifelong learners. What reading specialist candidates might expect in a preparation program and ideas for participating in a job interview for the reading specialist position are also offered.

## Reflections

Which type of learning—formal or informal—is most appealing to you, given where you are in your professional career? How can you take advantage of the opportunities that are available to you?

Think about the ideas suggested for those who are lifelong learners. Identify something you want to learn and develop a plan for doing so. Set a goal, develop a plan of action, set a deadline—and plan for a reward.

## Activities

1. Organize a study group in which you and several others agree to read and discuss a specific book that addresses an issue or problem in your school or setting.
2. Participate in a role-play of a job interview, using the questions in Appendix B.

# Appendix A

# The Roles of the Reading Specialist

Teaching all children to read requires that every child receive excellent reading instruction, and that children who are struggling with reading receive additional instruction from professionals specifically prepared to teach them. The range of student achievement found in classrooms, with the inclusion of children who have various physical, emotional, and educational needs, requires that we move to different educational models from those of the past. These new models present opportunities for teachers and reading specialists to work collaboratively to provide effective instruction for all students. In order to provide these services, schools must have reading specialists who can provide expert instruction, assessment, and leadership for the reading program.

## BUILDING THE CASE: WHY SPECIALISTS?

One of the many recommendations that comes from the report of the National Research Council, *Preventing Reading Difficulties in Young Children* (Snow, Burns, & Griffin, 1998), directly focuses on the need for in-school specialists "who have specialized training related to addressing reading difficulties and who can give guidance to classroom teachers" (p. 333). The report recommends that schools without reading specialists reexamine their needs, because reading specialists provide leadership and instructional expertise for the prevention and remediation of reading difficulties. These conclusions of the National Research Council, formed in response to a growing concern about the need to provide excellent instruction so that all children can become successful readers, are based on the Council's analysis of research on reading and reading instruction. Building on this foundation, this position statement (a) explains why teaching all children to read depends on reading specialists, (b) identifies reading specialists, (c) defines the roles of reading specialists, and (d) comments on the preparation of reading specialists.

Schools today face a complex and difficult challenge. Classrooms are filled with children with diverse needs, from those who are strong and healthy to those who have emotional, physical, and learning problems; to those who come from high poverty backgrounds or diverse cultural backgrounds; to those who are English language learners struggling with learning to read. These challenges and the need for high levels of literacy, given our technological society, are increasing the demand for a highly competent teacher workforce prepared to address these issues (National Commission on Teaching and America's Future, 1996). There is strong agreement that schools will succeed only when teachers have the expertise and competence needed to teach reading effectively (Pressley, 1998; Snow et al., 1998). Legislatures and teacher preparation institutions have increased the reading and language arts requirements for those who wish to become teachers, recognizing the need for expertise in this area. At the same time, there is recognition of the need for personnel with specialized knowledge about reading instruction who can provide essential services not only to students but to teachers whose diverse students present many challenges.

Where no instructional support exists, there appears to be an over-referral and inappropriate placement of children who have reading problems into special education programs (Allington & Walmsley, 1995). Many teachers feel overwhelmed with the tasks that face them, given the range of abilities and achievement in their classrooms. Too often, this daunting challenge leads to literacy instruction that might be improved with support from reading specialists.

There is also evidence that reading specialists are key factors in producing better reading achievement. Principals from exemplary schools that had reading specialists on staff indicated that these reading specialists were vital to the success of their reading programs (Bean, 1997). In Connecticut, two studies (Baron, 1999; Klein, Monti, Mulcahy-Ernt, & Speck, 1997) found that in comparable schools, students with reading consultants had higher reading test scores than those of students in schools without reading consultants. These results, along with the recommendation made by the National Research Council (Snow et al., 1998) about the importance of reading specialists, support the need for reading specialists as a means of enhancing students' reading performance.

## THE READING SPECIALIST

The reading specialist is a professional with advanced preparation and experience in reading who has responsibility (i.e., providing instruction, serving as a resource to teachers) for the literacy performance of readers in general and of struggling readers in particular. Such individuals may work at one or more of the following levels—early childhood, elementary, middle, secondary, or adult learners—and in various settings—public, private, or commercial schools; reading resource centers; or clinics.

The publication *Standards for Reading Professionals* (International Reading Association, 1998) provides a comprehensive list of proficiencies for the reading specialist. This list provides a baseline for thinking about reading specialists and how their roles differ from their roles in the past and from those of other literacy professionals. Specifically, reading specialists must possess the appropriate graduate education credentials, certificates, or degrees required by their state education body and demonstrate the proficiencies listed in the *Standards*. Although teachers may learn a great deal from taking various workshops or courses related to literacy, the role of specialist requires an integrated, sustained, and rigorous preparation program. To protect the integrity of the reading specialist position, all individuals in such a position should have advanced graduate preparation and appropriate educational credentials. Reading specialists should have prior classroom experience as a means of developing a more thorough understanding of classroom instruction and a better sense of and appreciation for the classroom teacher's role, as well as for establishing the credibility necessary for a reading specialist.

Although the majority of reading specialists work in elementary schools, these specialists also serve an important role in middle schools and secondary schools. At these levels, specialists must work with content teachers to assist them in building a better understanding of the relevance of reading to their discipline, how to use their textbooks effectively, and how to implement effective literary strategies. These specialists also need to be aware of how to help students become motivated, strategic, and independent learners.

Specialists involved in adult literacy will need to have a special understanding of their adult students as well as the proficiencies of all reading specialists. Adults bring to the instructional setting many problems and attitudes about reading that influence the nature of instruction.

Reading specialists also work in private reading clinics and community tutoring centers. In these settings, reading specialists should work closely with classroom teachers or volunteers to reinforce and support effective classroom instruction. It is important that students have a coherent and congruent reading program, and communication between those responsible for providing reading instruction is of critical importance.

## ROLES OF THE READING SPECIALIST

Reading specialists can assume multiple roles in schools, depending on the needs of the student population and teachers in the district. In fact, the role of the reading specialist can be seen on a continuum, with some specialists working primarily in a teaching role with students, while others spend the majority of their time in professional development with classroom teachers in a more formal leadership role. However, all specialists, regardless of role, must be involved in supporting the work of the classroom teacher and in developing the reading program so that it is effective for all students.

The major roles of reading specialists, each of which contributes to the improvement of student learning, are instruction, assessment, and leadership. The [accompanying figure] illustrates the synergistic nature of these roles; each contributes to the other and all contribute to increased learning for all students.

### Instruction

In the past, reading specialists have generally been viewed as educators who work with children who are struggling readers, supplementing or supplanting the work of the classroom teacher. Today, new roles are necessary. What appears to be most effective is for the reading specialist's instruction to support, supplement, and extend excellent classroom teaching (Pikulski, 1994. Such a view calls for the specialist and classroom teacher to work collaboratively to implement a quality reading program that is research-based and meets the needs of students. Then the classroom teacher and reading specialist can align instruction so that the teaching is congruent and of high quality (Allington & Walmsley 1995; Kennedy, Birman, & Demaline, 1986). These professionals can and must communicate with each other and with others (parents or other specialized personnel, such as the special education teacher or counselor) about instruction.

In order to promote congruency, collaboration, and communication between classroom teachers and reading specialists, the instruction provided by the reading specialist may take place in the classroom. This approach has merit because it stresses the importance of a coordinated instructional approach. On the other hand, there are programs in which the specialist provides instruction outside the classroom. This may occur when the child requires specialized and individualized instruction, for example, for Reading Recovery instruction. A well-coordinated, congruent, and quality program can occur whether the reading specialist functions in the classroom or in a pullout setting.

## Assessment

Reading specialists have specialized knowledge of assessment and diagnosis that is vital for developing, implementing, and evaluating the literacy program in general, and in designing instruction for individual students. Reading spe-

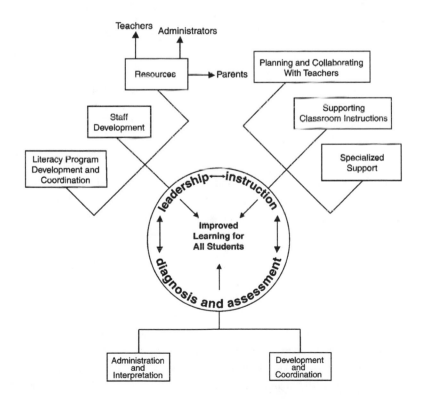

cialists can assess the reading strengths and needs of students and provide that information to classroom teachers, parents, and specialized personnel such as psychologists, special educators, or speech teachers in order to provide an effective reading program.

Such assessment does not necessarily require extensive formal testing. Rather, it may include observing the child in the classroom, discussing results of various classroom assessment measures with the teacher, or working with a child to determine how he or she responds to various literacy tasks. The specialist collaborates with the classroom teacher to use assessment results to plan and implement an appropriate reading program for the child.

Reading specialists also may have an important role in coordinating efforts related to district or state standards. These standards often require the development and implementation of various assessment tools. Specialists may need to work with teachers in the development of rubrics and alternative measures for assessing literacy and for instructional decision making. Moreover, reading specialists can be an important resource in assisting teachers in learning how to administer or interpret assessment results.

## Leadership

The leadership role is multidimensional. All reading specialists need to be a resource to other educators, parents, and the community. They also aid teachers by suggesting ideas, strategies, or materials that can enhance instruction. They play an essential role in supporting individual teachers—especially new teachers—and administrators in becoming more knowledgeable about the teaching of reading. They lead professional development workshops, model strategies or techniques for teachers, and conduct demonstration or collaborative lessons. They also serve as a resource to other specialized personnel by serving on instructional support or student personnel teams. They are aware of the characteristics of adult learners and they understand how learning proceeds across the life span, and they have excellent interpersonal skills. They have an important role in building good home–school connections, both through their work with parents and in helping teachers to establish effective parent–teacher relationships. The reading specialist also is involved in providing instructional guidance to aides, volunteers, tutors, or paraprofessionals who may be working in the classroom to assist the teacher in meeting the needs of students. Such guidance is critical, though frequently such personnel are not used appropriately.

Reading specialists have a strong influence on the overall reading program in the school. When schools designate reading specialists to assume this type of leadership role, there appears to be a strong, positive influence on the reading achievement of students (Klein et al., 1997). Such specialists become change agents who work with teachers to create total school reform. Specialists in this position have a major responsibility for coordinating and providing leadership for the schoolwide literacy program, including the selection of materials and the development of curriculum. They provide professional development for school staff so that teachers are aware of current strategies and techniques for teaching literacy. As leaders, reading specialists must know sources of funding that might be available to enhance the literacy program and be able to write proposals for obtaining such grants.

As school leaders, reading specialists must serve as advocates for the literacy program. They will need to communicate with many different audiences including school boards, parents, and community agencies. Thus, they must be able to articulate the schoolwide reading program to others. Some reading specialists also may be involved in teacher supervision, which necessitates skill in observing and conferring with teachers. These specialists often are designated as district reading supervisors or coordinators and have responsibility for evaluating the district reading program and its outcomes. They then may be responsible for professional development of other specialists on staff. Because so many reading specialist positions are funded by Title I, specialists in leadership positions may be responsible for administering the Title I program and for facilitating the work of other reading specialists in the district.

## PREPARING READING SPECIALISTS

*Standards for Reading Professionals* (1998) provides essential information about the qualifications necessary for reading specialists. The document requires that reading specialists, as well as all literacy professionals, have proficiency in three broad categories: knowledge and beliefs about reading, instruction and assessment, and organizing and enhancing a reading program. The document stresses the importance of knowledge and understanding of reading as well as the ability to communicate and collaborate with others so that such knowledge is transferred to classroom practice. As part of the specialist preparation program, reading specialists must complete a clinical practicum in which they work with students with reading difficulties. A practicum experience that includes working with adult learners also is recommended. Further, *Standards for Reading Professionals* also emphasizes the need for leadership capabilities, requiring institutions to include experiences that will enable specialist candidates to develop such skills. In the *Standards*, each of the major categories is described in depth so that institutions responsible for preparing reading specialists can obtain explicit information related to preparation.

## RECOMMENDATION

Given the U.S. agenda for improving the literacy performance of students and the increasing demands for educating all students to achieve at high levels, it is essential that schools have the personnel best prepared to address these challenges. Such personnel must include a qualified reading specialist as a core member of the educational team. The International Reading Association agrees with U.S. Secretary of Education Richard Riley, who stated, "Every elementary school should have the reading specialists they need to make a difference" (1999). To this, however, we would add that middle schools and high schools should have the same instructional support, because effective reading instruction must be guided by reading specialists across all grade levels.

## REFERENCES

Allington, R.L., & Walmsley, S.A. (1995). *No quick fix: Rethinking literacy programs in America's elementary schools.* New York: Teachers College Press; Newark, DE: International Reading Association.

Baron, J.B. (1999). *Exploring high and improving reading achievement in Connecticut.* Washington, DC: National Goals Panel.

Bean, R.M. (1997). *Reading specialists in exemplary schools* (unpublished document).

International Reading Association. (1998). *Standards for reading professionals—Revised.* Newark, DE: Author.

Kennedy, M., Birman, B.F., & Demaline, R.E. (1986). *The effectiveness of Chapter 1 services* (Second Interim Report for the National Assessment of Chapter 1). Washington, DC: Office of Educational Research and Improvement. (ERIC Document Reproduction Service No. ED281 919)

Klein, J., Monti, D., Mulcahy-Ernt P., & Speck, A. (1997). *Literacy for all: Reading/language arts programs and personnel in Connecticut schools.* Wethersfield: Connecticut Association for Reading Research.

National Commission on Teaching and America's Future. (1996). *What matters most: Teaching for America's future.* New York: Teachers College Press.

Pikulski, J.J. (1994). Preventing reading failure: A review of five effective programs. *The Reading Teacher, 48,* 30–39.

Pressley, M. (1998). *Reading instruction that works: The case for balanced teaching.* New York: Guilford Press.

Riley, R.W. (1999, February 16). Sixth annual state of American education speech [Online]. Available: *http://www.ed.gov/Speeches/02-1999/990216-a.html.*

Snow, C.E., Burns, M.S., & Griffin, P. (Eds.). (1998). *Preventing reading difficulties in young children.* Washington, DC: National Academy Press.

## RELATED RESOURCES AVAILABLE FROM THE INTERNATIONAL READING ASSOCIATION

*Building a Knowledge Base in Reading*
Jane Braunger, Jan Patricia Lewis 1997

*Literacy Instruction for Culturally and Linguistically Diverse Students: A Collection of Articles and Commentaries*
Michael F. Opitz, Editor 1998

*Starting Out Right: A Guide to Promoting Children's Reading Success*
M. Susan Burns, Peg Griffin, Catherine E. Snow, Editors 1999

*Struggling Adolescent Readers: A Collection of Teaching Strategies*
David W. Moore, Donna E. Alvermann, Kathleen A. Hinchman, Editors 2000

*Teaching Struggling Readers: Articles from* The Reading Teacher
Richard L. Allington, Editor 1998

*Using the Knowledge Base in Reading: Teachers at Work*
Jane Braunger, Jan Patricia Lewis 1999

*Variability Not Disability: Struggling Readers in a Workshop Classroom*
Cathy M. Roller 1996

**Adopted by the Board of Directors, January 2000**
*Board of Directors at Time of Adoption*

Carol Minnick Santa, President
Carmelita K. Williams, President-Elect
Donna Ogle, Vice President
Alan E. Farstrup, Executive Director

Kathryn H. Au
Betsy M. Baker
Patricia A. Edwards
Adria F. Klein
Gregg M. Kurek
Diane L. Larson
Jeanne R. Paratore
Lori L. Rog
Timothy Shanahan

# Appendix B

## Preparation for Job Interviews

Candidates for positions as reading specialists often raise questions regarding how they can prepare for job interviews. The questions identified below are some that may be asked by school personnel. Often interviewers ask basic questions to get a sense of the experiences and education of candidates. In addition, they ask questions that elicit candidates' beliefs and perspectives regarding students, literacy teaching, and learning. These questions tend to be more difficult to answer because the interviewer probably has his or her own beliefs and values regarding each area. Be as honest and tactful as possible. The interviewer needs to know whether the reading specialist is a "match" for the district. At the same time, the reading specialist needs to determine whether the district is a place in which he or she will enjoy working.

### BASIC QUESTIONS

1. Tell us about your past teaching experiences, especially those that prepare you for this position.
2. What certifications do you have? Where did you receive your reading specialist certification? What were the strengths of the program?

## QUESTIONS ELICITING KNOWLEDGE, BELIEFS, AND UNDERSTANDINGS

1. What are your beliefs about reading instruction? Specifically, what are your beliefs about beginning reading instruction? Phonics instruction (primary position)? What are your beliefs about intermediate reading instruction? Secondary reading instruction?
2. What assessment instruments have you had experience administering and interpreting? Talk about them and their possible uses.
3. What do you think about pullout and in-class reading programs? Is one better than the other? Why?
4. What do you think is important in working effectively with teachers whose students you will be teaching? Why?
5. In addition to teaching struggling readers, what other kinds of contributions can you make to the reading program?
6. Have you had any experience in conducting professional development? If so, what?
7. What strengths (qualifications) do you think you would bring to this position? Why do you want this position?

## QUESTIONS THE READING SPECIALIST SHOULD ASK

The interview should also provide an opportunity for the reading specialist to obtain information about the position. Interviewers often ask if the interviewee has any questions, so the reading specialist should go into the interview with several questions important to him or her. Broad categories of topics follow:

1. *Duties required:* What are the expectations of the position regarding teaching, assessment, etc.?
2. *Resources:* What materials and resources are available for teaching reading?
3. *Opportunities for collaboration:* In what ways can I collaborate with teachers, parents, community entities such as libraries, etc.?
4. *Professional opportunities:* Does the district encourage continuing education and provide opportunities for teachers to attend conferences?

The following guidelines might also be helpful in an interview.

1. *Listen carefully before answering any question.* Be certain you know what is being asked.

2. *Answer questions honestly.* If you do not know a specific answer, it is best to say so (or qualify your answer by saying that you are not certain, but to the best of your ability, you think . . .).

3. *Show enthusiasm and interest in the position.* Indicate why you want to work in that specific school and why you believe you would be an excellent candidate for the job.

# References

Alexander, K. L., Entwisle, D. R., & Olson, L. S. (2001). Schools, achievement, and inequality: A seasonal perspective. *Educational Evaluation and Policy Analysis, 23*(2), 171–191.

Alexander, S. H. (1990). *Mom can't see me.* New York: Macmillan.

Allington, R. L. (1986). Policy constraints and effective compensatory reading instruction: A review. In J. Hoffman (Ed.), *Effective teaching of reading and research and practice* (pp. 261–289). Newark, DE: International Reading Association.

Allington, R. L., & Baker, K. (1999). Best practices in literacy instruction for children with special needs. In L. B. Gambrell, L. M. Morrow, S. B. Neuman, & M. Pressley (Eds.), *Best practices in literacy instruction* (pp. 292–310). New York: Guilford Press.

Allington, R. L., & McGill-Franzen, A. (1989). School response to reading failure: Instruction for chapter 1 and special education students in grades 2, 4, and 8. *Elementary School Journal, 89*, 529–542.

Allington, R. L., & Shake, M. C. (1986). Remedial reading: Achieving curricular congruence in classroom and clinic. *The Reading Teacher, 39*(7), 648–654.

Alvermann, D. E. (2002). Effective literacy instruction for adolescents. *Journal of Literacy Research, 34*(2), 189–208.

Alvermann, D. E., & Phelps, S. F. (2002). *Content reading and literacy: Succeeding in today's diverse classrooms* (3rd ed.). Boston: Allyn & Bacon.

Anonymous. (1986). Where have all the children gone? *Scanner, Shaler Area Education Association, 13*(2), 3.

Armbruster, B. B., & Osborn J. (2001). *Put reading first: The research building blocks for teaching children to read.* Washington, DC: National Institute for Literacy and the Partnership for Reading.

Au, K. (2001). *Elementary programs: Guiding change in a time of standards.* In S. B. Wepner, D. S. Strickland, & J. T. Feeley (Eds.), *The administration and supervision of reading programs* (3d ed., pp. 42–58). New York: Teachers College Press.

Bader, L. A. (1998). *Read to succeed: Literacy tutor's manual.* Upper Saddle River, NJ: Prentice-Hall.

Baker, S., Gersten, R., & Keating, T. (2000). When less may be more: A 2-year longitudinal evaluation of a volunteer tutoring program requiring minimal training. *Reading Research Quarterly, 35*(4), 494–519.

Barnett, W. S. (1995). Long-term effects of early childhood programs on cognitive and school outcomes. *The Future of Children, 5*(3), 25–50.

Barnett, W. S., Frede, E. C., Mobasher, H., & Mohr, P. (1987). The efficacy of public preschool programs and the relationship of program quality to efficacy. *Educational Evaluation and Policy Analysis, 10*(1), 37–49.

Bean, R. M. (2001). Classroom teachers and reading specialists working together to improve student achievement. In V. Risko & K. Bromley (Eds.), *Collaboration for diverse learners: Viewpoints and practices* (pp. 348–368). Newark, DE: International Reading Association.

Bean, R. M. (2002). Developing an effective reading program. In S. B. Wepner, D. S. Strickland, & J. T. Feeley (Eds.), *The administration and supervision of reading programs* (3rd ed., pp. 3–15). New York: Teachers College Press.

Bean, R. M., Cassidy, J., Grumet, J. V., Shelton, D., & Wallis, S. R. (2002). What do reading specialists do? Results from a national survey. *The Reading Teacher, 55*(8), 2–10.

Bean, R. M., Cooley, W., Eichelberger, R. T., Lazar, M., & Zigmond, N. (1991). In-class or pullout: Effects of setting on the remedial reading program. *Journal of Reading Behavior, 23*(4), 445–464.

Bean, R. M., Eichelberger, R. T., Turner, G., & Tellez, F. (2002). *Evaluation of four parochial elementary schools.* Pittsburgh, PA: Extra Mile Foundation.

Bean, R. M., Grumet, J. V., & Bulazo, J. (1999). Learning from each other: Collaboration between classroom teachers and reading specialist interns. *Reading Research and Instruction, 38*(4), 273–287.

Bean, R. M., Swan, A. L., & Knaub, R. (2003). Reading specialists in schools with exemplary reading programs: Functional, versatile, and prepared. *The Reading Teacher, 56*(5), 446–455.

Bean, R. M., Swan, A. L., & Morris, G. (2003). *Providing professional development for teachers of beginning reading: Tinkering or transforming?* Manuscript submitted for publication.

Bean, R. M., Trovato, C. A., & Hamilton, R. (1995). Focus on Chapter 1 reading programs: Views of reading specialists, classroom teachers, and principals. *Reading Research and Instruction, 34*(3), 204–221.

Bean, R. M., Turner, G. H., & Belski, K. (2003). Implementing a successful America reads challenge tutoring program: Lessons learned. In P. E. Linder, M. B. Sampson, J. Dugan, & B. Brancato (Eds.), *24th Yearbook of the College Reading Association* (pp. 169–187). Easton, PA: College Reading Association.

Bean, R. M., & Wilson, R. M. (1981). *Effecting change in school reading programs: The resource role.* Newark, DE: International Reading Association.

Beck, I. L., & Hamilton, R. (1996). *Beginning reading module.* Washington, DC: American Federation of Teachers.

Beresik, D. L., & Bean, R. M. (2002). Teacher practices and the Pennsylvania system of school assessment. *Pennsylvania Reads: Journal of the Keystone State Reading Association, III*(II), 16–29.

Billig, S. H. (2002). Involving middle-graders' parents. *Education Digest, 67*(7), 42–45.

Blanchard, K., Bowles, S., Carew, D., & Parise-Carew, E. (2001). *High five: The magic of working together.* New York: HarperCollins.

Block, C. C., & Pressley, M. (Eds.). (2002). *Comprehension instruction: Research-based best practices.* New York: Guilford Press.

Borman, G. D. (2002–2003). How can Title 1 improve achievement? *Educational Leadership, 60*(4), 49–53.

Borman, G. D., & D'Agostine, J. V. (2001). Title 1 and student achievement: A quantitative synthesis. In G. D. Borman, S. C. Stringfield, & R. E. Slavin (Eds.), *Title I compensatory education at the crossroads* (pp. 25–58). Mahwah, NJ: Erlbaum.

Briggs, D. A., & Coulter F. C. (1977). The reading specialist. In W. Otto, N. A. Peters, & C. W. Peters, *Reading problems: A multidisciplinary perspective* (pp. 215–236). Reading, MA: Addison-Wesley.

Buehl, D. (2001). *Classroom strategies for interactive learning* (2nd ed.). Newark, DE: International Reading Association.

Cattagni, A., & Farris, E. (2001). Internet access in public schools and classrooms, 1994–2000 [Online]. *Education Statistics Quarterly: Elementary and secondary education.* Available: *http://nces.ed.gov/pbs2001/quarterly/summer/q2-7.asp*

Center for the Improvement of Early Reading Achievement (CIERA). (1998). *Every child a reader: Applying reading research in the classroom* [Online]. Ann Arbor, MI: Author. Available: *http://www.learningfirst.org/publications.html*

Clay, M. (1985). *The early detection of reading difficulties* (3rd ed.). Portsmouth, NH: Heinemann.

Cochran-Smith, M., & Lytle, S. L. (1993). *Inside/outside: Teacher research and knowledge.* New York: Teachers College Press.

Cook, L., & Friend, M. (1995). Co-teaching: Guidelines for creating effective practices. *Exceptional Children, 28*(3), 1–16.

Costa, A. L., & Garmston, R. J. (1994). *Cognitive coaching: A foundation for Renaissance schools* (2nd ed.). Norwood, MA: Christopher-Gordon.

Covey, S. (1989). *The 7 habits of highly effective people.* New York: Simon & Schuster.

Cunningham, P. M., & Hall, D. P. (1994). *Making words.* Torrance, CA: Good Apple.

Duke, N. K. (2000). 3.6 minutes per day: The scarcity of informational texts in first grade. *Reading Research Quarterly, 35*(2), 202–224.

Elbaum, B., Vaughn, S., Hughes, M. T., & Moody, S. W. (2000). How effective are one-to-one tutoring programs in reading for elementary students at risk for reading failure?: A meta-analysis of the intervention research. *Journal of Educational Psychology, 92*(4), 605–619.

Epstein, J. (1995). School/family community partnerships: Caring for the children we share. *Phi Delta Kappan, 76*(9), 701–712.

Farkas, G., Warren, M., & Johnson, A. (July, 1999). *Tutor manual: Reading one-to-one.* Dallas: University of Texas at Dallas, Center for Education and Social Policy, School of Social Sciences.

Farstrup, A. E., & Samuels, S. J. (2002). *What research has to say about reading instruction.* Newark, De: International Reading Association.

Fawson, P. C., & Reutzel, D. R. (2000). But I only have a basal: Implementing guided reading in the early grades. *The Reading Teacher, 54,* 84–97.

Fitzgerald, J. (2001). Can minimally trained college student volunteers help young at-risk children to read better? *Reading Research Quarterly, 36*(1), 28–47.

Fullan, M. (1991). *The new meaning of educational change.* New York: Teachers College Press.

Fullan, M., & Hargreaves, A. (1996). *What's worth fighting for in your school?* New York: Teachers College Press.

Glazer, S. M. (1998). *Assessment IS instruction: Reading, writing, spelling, and phonics for ALL learners.* Norwood, MA: Christopher-Gordon.

Glickman, C. D. (1990). *Supervision of instruction: A developmental approach.* Boston: Allyn & Bacon.

Good, (1973). *Dictionary of education* (3rd ed.). New York: McGraw Hill.

Guskey, T. R. (2000). *Evaluating professional development.* Thousand Oaks, CA: Corwin Press.

Guskey, T. R. (1986). Staff development and the process of teacher change. *Educational Researcher, 15*(5), 5–12.

Hall, G. E., & Hord, S. M. (1987). *Change in schools: Facilitating the process.* Albany: State University of New York Press.

Hamilton, R. L. (1993). *Chapter I reading instruction: Exemplary reading specialists in an in-class model.* Unpublished dissertation, University of Pittsburgh.

Hansen, J. (1998). *When learners evaluate.* Portsmouth, NH: Heinemann.

Harari, O. (2002). *The leadership secrets of Colin Powell.* New York: McGraw Hill.

Henderson, A., & Berla, N. (1995). *The family is critical to students' achievement* (2nd ed.). Washington, DC: Center for Law and Education.

Henk, W. A., Moore, J. C., Marinak, B. A., & Tomasetti, B. W. (2000). A reading lesson observation framework for elementary teachers, principals, and literacy supervisors. *The Reading Teacher, 53*(5), 358–369.

Henwood, G. F. (1999–2000). A new role for the reading specialist: Contributing toward a high school's collaborative educational culture. *Journal of Adolescent and Adult Literacy, 43*(4), 316–325.

Hersey, P., & Blanchard, K. (1977). *Management of organizational behavior: utilizing human resources* (3rd ed.). Englewood Cliffs, NJ: Prentice-Hall.

Hoffman, A. R., & Jenkins, J. (2002). Exploring reading specialists' collaborative interactions with school psychologists: Problems and possibilities. *Education, 122*(4), 751–758.

Hoffman, J. V., McCarthy, S. J., Elliott, B., Bayles, D. L., Price, D. P., Ferree, A., & Abbott, J. A. (1998). The literature-based basals in first grade classrooms: Savior, Satan, or same-old, same-old? *Reading Research Quarterly, 33*, 168–197.

International Reading Association. (1968). *Guidelines for reading specialists.* Newark, DE: Author.

International Reading Association. (1998). *Standards for reading professionals.* Newark, DE: Author.

International Reading Association. (1999). *Adolescent literacy: A position statement.* Newark, DE: Author.

International Reading Association. (2000). *Teaching all children to read: The roles of the reading specialist.* Newark, DE: Author.

International Reading Association. (2002a). *Buyer be wary: A resolution of IRA Board* [Online]. Available: www.reading.org

International Reading Association. (2002b). *Evidenced-based reading instruction: Putting the National Reading Panel Report into practice.* Newark, DE: Author.

International Reading Association and National Council of Teachers of English. (1996). *Standards for English language arts.* Newark, DE: Author.

International Society for Technology in Education. (2000). *National educational technology standards for students: Connecting curriculum and technology.* Eugene, OR: Author.

Irwin, J. (2002). *Facilitator's guide to IRA literacy study groups.* Newark, DE: International Reading Association.

Jacobs, H. H. (1997). *Mapping the big picture integrating curriculum and assessment K–12.* Washington, DC: Association for Supervision and Curriculum Development.

Johnson, D. W., & Johnson, F. P. (2003). *Joining together: Group theory and group skills* (8th ed.). Boston: Allyn & Bacon.

Johnston, F., Juel, C., & Invernizzi, M. (1995). *Guidelines for volunteer tutors of emergent and early readers.* Charlottesville: University of Virginia.

Jolles, R. L. (2001). *How to run seminars and workshops* (2nd ed.). New York: Wiley.

Joyce, B., & Showers, B. (1995). *Student achievement through staff development: Fundamentals of school renewal.* White Plains, NY: Longman.

Kamil, M. L., Mosenthal, P. B., Pearson, P. D., & Barr, R. (Eds.). (2000). *Handbook of reading research* (Vol. 3). Mahwah, NJ: Erlbaum.

Kaser, J., Mundry, S., Stiles, K. E., & Loucks-Horsley, S. (2002). *Leading every day: 124 actions for effective leadership.* Thousand Oaks, CA: Corwin Press.

Keene, E. L., & Zimmerman, S. (1997). *Mosaic of thought.* Portsmouth, NH: Heinemann.

Knaub, R. (2002). *The nature and impact of collaboration between reading specialists and classroom teachers in pullout and in-class reading programs.* Unpublished doctoral dissertation, University of Pittsburgh.

Kober, N. (2002, November). What tests can and cannot tell us. *The Forum,* pp. 1–2, 11–16.

Lambert, L. (1998). *Building leadership capacity in schools.* Alexandria, VA: Association for Supervision and Curriculum Development.

Lapp, D., Fisher, D., Flood, J., & Frey, N. (2003). Dual role of the urban reading specialist, *Journal of Staff Development, 24*(2), 33–36.

Lapp, D., Fisher, D., Flood, J., Goss-Moore, K., & Moore, J. (2002). Selecting materials for the literacy program. In S. B. Wepner, D. S. Strickland, & J. T. Feeley (Eds.), *The administration and supervision of reading programs* (3rd ed., pp. 83–94). New York: Teachers College Press.

Little, J. W. (1993). Teachers' professional development in a climate of education reform. *Educational Evaluation and Policy Analysis, 15* 129–151.

Lyons, C. A., & Pinnell, G. S. (2001). *Systems for change in literacy education: A guide to professional development.* Portsmouth, NH: Heinemann.

McVee, M. B., & Dickson, B. A. (2002). Creating a rubric to examine literacy software for the primary grades. *The Reading Teacher, 55*(7), 635–639.

Moats, L. (1999). *Teaching reading is rocket science: What expert teachers of reading should know and be able to do* [Online]. Washington, DC: American Federation of Teachers. Available: *http://www.aft.org*

Morrow, L. M., & Woo, D. G. (Eds.). (2000). *Tutoring programs for struggling readers: The America Reads challenge.* New York: Guilford Press.

National Center for Educational Statistics (NCES). (1996). *Parents and schools: Partners in student learning.* Washington, DC: Author.

National Center for Educational Statistics (NCES). (1998). *Parent involvement in children's education: Efforts by public elementary schools.* Washington, DC: Author.

National Institute of Child Health and Human Development. (2000). *Report of the National Reading Panel. Teaching children to read: An evidence-based assessment of the scientific research literature on reading and its implications for reading instruction* (NIH Publication No. 00-4769). Washington, DC: U.S. Government Printing Office. Available: *http://www.nationalreadingpanel.org/*

*Publications/subgroups* (This document can be downloaded or ordered from the National Institute for Literacy at ED Pubs, 800-228-8813.)

National Institute for Literacy/National Institute of Child Health and Human Development/U.S. Department of Education. (2003). *Adolescent literacy: Research informing practice* [Online]. Washington, DC: Author. Available: *http://www/nifl.gov/partnershipforreading/ adolescent/overview.html 2/4/2003*

National Staff Development Council. (2001). *Standards for staff development* [Online]. Oxford, OH: Author. Available: *http://www.nsdc.org*

Neuman, S. B., & Dickinson, D. K. (Eds.). (2001). *Handbook of early literacy research.* New York: Guilford Press.

Ogle, D. (1986). K-W-L: A teaching model that develops active reading of expository text. *The Reading Teacher, 39,* 564–572.

Ogle, D., & Fogelberg, E. (2001). Expanding collaborative roles of reading specialists: Developing an intermediate reading support team. In V. Risko & K. Bromley (Eds.), *Collaboration for diverse learners: Viewpoints and practices* (pp. 152–167). Newark, DE: International Reading Association.

Pennsylvania Department of Education. (2002, September). *Grade 3 Reading Assessment Rubric, preliminary version* [Online]. Available: *http://www. pde.state.pa.us/a_and_t/lib/a_and_t/Grade3ReadingRubricSeptember2002. pdf*

Pikulski, J. (1994). Preventing reading failure: A review of five effective programs. *The Reading Teacher, 48,* 30–39.

Pressley, M. (2002). Effective beginning reading instruction. *Journal of Literacy Research, 34*(2), 165–188.

Quatroche, D. J., Bean, R. M., & Hamilton, R. L. (2001). The role of the reading specialist: A review of research. *The Reading Teacher, 55*(3), 282–294.

Richek, M. A., Caldwell, J., Jennings, J., & Lerner, J. (2002). *Reading problems: Assessment and teaching strategies* (4th ed.). Boston: Allyn & Bacon.

Robbins, P. (1991). *How to implement a peer coaching program.* Washington, DC: Association for Supervision and Curriculum Development.

Sackor, S. (2001). *Three-to-one tutoring: Strategies to enhance the reading comprehension of poor intermediate readers.* Unpublished dissertation, University of Pittsburgh.

Sanders, W. L., & Horn, S. P. (1994). The Tennessee Value-Added Assessment System (TVAAS): Mixed-model methodology in educational assessment. *Journal of Personnel Evaluation in Education, 8*(3), 299–311.

Sanders, W. L., & Rivers, J. C. (1996). *Cumulative and residual effects of teachers on future student academic achievement.* Knoxville: University of Tennessee Value-Added Research and Assessment Center.

Schumm, J. S., & Mangrum, C. T. (1991). FLIP: A framework for fostering textbook thinking. *Journal of Reading, 35,* 120–124.

Sendak, M. (1988). *Where the wild things are.* New York: Harper & Row.

Simmons, D. C., & Kame'enui, E. T. (2002). *A consumer's guide to evaluating a core reading program grades K–3: A critical elements analysis.* Eugene: University of Oregon, National Center to Improve the Tools of Educators and Institute for the Development of Educational Achievement.

Slavin, R. E. (1987). Making Chapter 1 make a difference. *Phi Delta Kappan, 69*(2), 110–119.

Slavin, R. E., Madden, N. A., Dolan, L. J., & Wasik, B. A. (1996). *Every child, every school success for all.* Thousand Oaks, CA: Corwin Press.

Snow, C., Burns, M. S., & Griffin, P. (Eds.). (1998). *Preventing reading difficulties in young children.* Washington, DC: National Research Council.

Stauffer, R. G. (1967). Change, BUT—. *The Reading Teacher, 20,* 474–499.

Stephens, L. (2000). *Internet usage in public schools* (4th ed.). Denver, CO: Quality Education Data.

Strickland, D. S., & Morrow, L. M. (2000). *Beginning reading and writing.* New York: Teachers College Press.

Taylor, B. M., & Pearson, P. D. (2002). The CIERA school change classroom observation scheme. Minneapolis: University of Minnesota.

Taylor, B. M., Pressley, M., & Pearson, P. D. (2002). Research-supported characteristics of teachers and schools that promote reading achievement. In B. M. Taylor & M. Pearson (Eds.), *Teaching reading: Effective schools, accomplished teachers* (pp. 361–374). NJ: Erlbaum.

Thomas, A., Fazio, L., & Stiefelmeyer, B. L. (1999). *Families at school: A guide for educators.* Newark, DE: International Reading Association.

Thomas, A., Fazio, L., & Stiefelmeyer, B. L. (1999). *Families at school: A handbook for parents.* Newark, DE: International Reading Association.

Tierney, R. J., Johnston, P., Moore, D. W., & Valencia, S. W. (2000). Snippets: How will literacy be assessed in the next millennium? *Reading Research Quarterly, 35*(4), 244–250.

Walp, T. P., & Walmsley, S. A. (1989). Instructional and philosophical congruence: Neglected aspects of coordination. *The Reading Teacher, 42*(6), 364–368.

Wasik, B. A. (1998). Volunteer tutoring programs in reading: A review. *Reading Research Quarterly, 33,* 266–292.

Wasik, B. A., & Slavin, R. E. (1993). Preventing early reading failure with one-to-one tutoring: A review of five programs. *Reading Research Quarterly, 28*(2), 178–200.

Weber, E. (1999). *Student assessment that works: A practical approach.* Boston: Allyn & Bacon.

# Index